Structured Finance in Latin America

Structured Finance in Latin America

Channeling Pension Funds to Housing, Infrastructure, and Small Businesses

Hela Cheikhrouhou
W. Britt Gwinner
John Pollner
Emanuel Salinas
Sophie Sirtaine
Dimitri Vittas

THE WORLD BANK
Washington, D.C.

©2007 The International Bank for Reconstruction and Development / The World Bank
1818 H Street NW
Washington DC 20433
Telephone: 202-473-1000
Internet: www.worldbank.org
E-mail: feedback@worldbank.org

ISBN-10: 0-8213-7139-8
ISBN-13: 978-0-8213-7139-8
eISBN-10: 0-8213-7140-1
eISBN-13: 978-0-8213-7140-4

Cover photo: World Bank Photo Library.

Library of Congress Cataloging-in-Publication Data

Structured finance in Latin America : channeling pension funds to housing, infrastructure, and small businesses / Hela Cheikhrouhou . . . [et al.]
        p. cm.
        Includes bibliographical references and index.
    ISBN-13: 978-0-8213-7139-8
    ISBN-10: 0-8213-7139-8
    ISBN-13: 978-0-8213-7140-4 (electronic)
    ISBN-10: 0-8213-7140-1 (electronic)
    1. Pension trusts—Investments—Latin America. 2. Housing—Latin America—Finance.
3. Infrastructure (Economics)—Latin America—Finance. 4. Small business—Latin
America—Finance. I. Cheikhrouhou, Hela, 1972– II. World Bank.
    HD7105.45.L29S87 2007
    332.67'264098—dc22
                                                            2007019040

Contents

Boxes

Figures

Tables

Acknowledgments

This report was prepared by a team led by Hela Cheikhrouhou and comprising W. Britt Gwinner (housing finance), John Pollner (pensions), Emanuel Salinas (small and medium enterprises), Sophie Sirtaine (infrastructure), and Dimitri Vittas (pensions and framework). Valuable contributions were received from Mariluz Cortes, Luis De La Plaza, Radwa El-Swaify, and Sarah Zekri. The peer reviewers of the overall report were Stijn Claessens and Allison Harwood, with topic-specific reviewers Loic Chiquier, Severine Dinghem, Leora Klapper, and Heinz Rudolph. The team would like to thank Augusto de la Torre for valuable comments. The report was edited by Communications Development Incorporated.

Executive Summary

The introduction of fully funded private pension systems in several countries in Latin America and the Caribbean is leading to rapid asset accumulation by institutional investors. Initially, it has been the private pension funds (*administradoras de fondos de pensión*, or AFPs), set up as defined contribution plans to supplement or replace public defined benefit systems, that have been accumulating assets most rapidly. As the systems mature into the payout phase, however, the assets will shift to annuity providers, typically life insurers.

The largest asset class held by AFPs is government securities, largely because of restrictive investment regulations and the lack of high-quality private securities. This limits the returns on AFP investments and leads to low and volatile wage replacement rates (ratio of pension to final wages) for retirees. Meanwhile, there are large financing needs in residential housing, infrastructure projects, and small and medium enterprises (SMEs) that are not being met by the banking system. Innovative structured financing can channel more resources from institutional investors to these underserved sectors by boosting the creditworthiness of the securities issued in these sectors. Structured securities would help to bridge the gap between credit offered and credit demanded and to develop incomplete financial markets.

Despite greater stability and improved performance, the financial sectors in Latin American countries are not contributing to social and economic development as much as had been expected when reforms were instituted (de la Torre, Gozzi, and Schmukler 2006). Over the past quarter of a century, financial sector policies in Latin American countries have focused on shifting to market-based financial systems and converging toward international standards promoting financial stability. This emphasis has produced several positive outcomes, including tremendous gains in macroeconomic stability and in prudential regulation of banks, creating a favorable environment for longer-term investments. Several countries have made important advances in the infrastructure and regulation of capital markets and, to a lesser extent, in the growth of local currency debt markets. Also, as local financial systems have grown, they have become better integrated into international markets. However, the contractual and creditor rights environment is still incomplete, local stock markets remain small in most Latin American countries, and bank credit is accessible mainly to large corporations and higher-income households. The challenge is to deepen financial intermediation to meet the financing needs of underserved segments—in particular, to increase housing finance, which is picking up in some countries, but still remains grossly inadequate; to finance growing needs for infrastructure; and to meet the finance needs of SMEs, which remain the least well-served.

The accumulation of long-term savings in countries that have adopted defined contribution pension plans provides an opportunity to channel more financial resources to underserved sectors. AFPs (and increasingly annuity providers) are accumulating long-term savings, which are crucial to deepening financial intermediation and transforming resources into viable long-term investments, especially for housing and infrastructure finance.

AFPs are growing fast in several Latin American countries, and annuity providers will start to grow as the fully funded pension systems mature. As of December 2005, Latin America's AFPs had more than US$300 billion in assets under management, or about 10–15 percent of gross domestic product (GDP) in countries where reforms were fairly recent and close to 60 percent in Chile (excluding annuity providers), the first country to move to a defined contribution scheme. Other Latin American countries that kept a parallel defined benefit pillar may not achieve such large fully funded pensions, even when their systems mature, but AFPs (and soon annuity providers) are sizable and growing fast in these countries as well. They are an important class of domestic investors and a large source of capital for highly creditworthy investments.

Structured finance (particularly securitization) can help with the large financing needs of underserved sectors in Latin American countries. Structured finance involves the pooling of assets and the subsequent sale to institutional investors of claims on the cash flows backed by these pools. An important characteristic of this type of finance is the delinking of the collateral assets pool from the credit risk of the originator, usually through the use of a special purpose vehicle. The report covers several types of structured finance with such capital market instruments as mortgage-backed securities, structured bond issues for infrastructure financing, securitization of SME-related assets, and securitization of loans to SMEs. The report also covers factoring and leasing, which can be important sources of finance for SMEs and can be pooled and packaged into marketable securities and sold to pension funds. The report does not cover other types of structured finance, such as exchange trade funds, structured notes with capital protection, or structured financing outside capital markets, such as bank syndications.

Fast-Growing Private Pension Funds (and Emerging Annuity Providers) Have Constraints on Investing Their Assets

Government debt is typically the largest asset class held by AFPs (and annuity providers) and will remain so, especially where the pension reform was costly and financed by debt. Pension reforms have increased the need for government issuance of debt, and the growth of debt has depended on the reform design—on whether it was mostly debt or tax financed and on how generous the defined benefit public scheme and the transition arrangements were. In the early stages of reform, several countries required that a significant percentage of AFP assets be invested in government securities.[1] These securities are considered risk-free assets, with the highest domestic credit rating (AAA) and a 0 percent risk-adjusted equity requirement. This enhanced the appetite of institutional investors for government securities and crowded out private issuers, leaving an average investment in government debt of 70 percent across Latin American countries.

Despite complex regulations and incentives, AFPs (and annuity providers) have an appetite for diversifying assets and enhancing returns. Misaligned incentives, especially for AFPs, include weak correlation between fund returns and the financial performance of the administrator (or its staff), the nature of AFPs as pure asset managers, the limited competition based on returns, the presence of minimum return guarantees, and industry-wide herding effects. Even so, AFPs (and annuity providers) seek investments that complement government debt, given the rapid pace of their asset growth and the historical lows that risk-free real returns are approaching.

AFPs (and annuity providers) display a high aversion to credit risk, due to their mandate and a weak creditor rights environment. As entities managing the old-age income of workers, AFPs are rightly required to invest in highly creditworthy securities. The usual threshold is domestic investment grade (BBB+). Yet AFPs have proven more conservative, typically investing only in AAA and some AA securities, almost never going down to A or BBB because of worries about local contractual enforcement, creditor rights, bankruptcy and insolvency procedures, and credit information and registry systems. In addition, some countries restrict the AFPs' ability to hold securities that have to be restructured over their life or to continue to hold securities that have been downgraded below investment grade, which can lead to larger credit losses due to forced liquidation. So, the cost of going down a notch can be large.

AFPs typically have a strict limit on investing abroad. Constraints on foreign investment abroad—typically held to no more than 20 percent, but varying across countries from 0 to 50 percent—restrict the capacity to tap into the wide variety of highly creditworthy international securities. This forces funds to seek opportunities locally and may artificially lower the returns and spreads required by institutional investors.

Local capital markets are lackluster. Domestic stock and bond markets have not kept pace with the rapid growth of institutional investors. De la Torre and Schmukler (2004) document the growing internationalization of stock issuance by large Latin American firms and the limited scope of fixed-income markets (see appendix 2 for statistics).

The supply of high-quality private sector securities is particularly inadequate. The number of domestic issuers of AAA and AA securities is limited. In addition to investing in governmental entities, AFPs (and annuity providers) in Latin American countries invest in domestic financial sector securities (especially banking) and structured deposit products. But their appetite for financial sector exposure has its limits because of the need to diversify and to avoid systemic banking risk. Institutional investors also seek securities of the nonfinancial private sector.

The corporate sector in Latin America and the Caribbean—and all emerging market economies—is pyramidal, with a broad base and a tight top. Many large companies are owned by multinationals, which raise part of their financing internationally. In many countries, several of the top-tier local corporations may not be AAA or AA, they may be adequately and flexibly serviced by domestic banks, or they may not want to apply the governance and disclosure standards demanded by capital markets. But many larger enterprises have benefited from institutional investors' aggressive search for new issuers, pushing local banks down-market to seek alternative niches. These niches have so far been in the consumer lending, housing, and, more recently, microcredit sectors. SMEs have been slower to benefit from this move—due partly to structural issues in creditor rights enforcement and difficulties in applying credit scoring and a portfolio approach.

Institutional investors' need for a minimum issue size further restricts the universe of potential domestic issuers. AFPs (and annuity providers) have an administrative cost structure that precludes analyzing large numbers of small individual investments.[2] They are also subject to concentration limits by issuer and issue, so an individual issuance needs to be fairly large to be palatable to institutional investors.

But institutional investors have a unique capacity to take on market risks to enhance their returns. AFPs (and annuity providers) have proven to have more appetite than mutual funds or banks to take on low-liquidity, long-maturity, long-duration, local currency, and inflation-indexed investments as a way to enhance returns through market risk rather than credit risk or to hedge particular exposures (long-dated liabilities of annuity providers). AFPs can more easily seek enhanced returns through an illiquidity premium and positive carry on the yield curve than through more credit risk. Unlike banks and mutual funds, AFPs (and annuity providers) do not face runs on deposits,[3] and they expect the growth in their assets under management to continue over the medium term.

Financial Engineering Can Help Meet the Particular Requirements of Institutional Investors

Structured financing is tailored debt financing that meets issuer or investor needs that standard financial products cannot meet. The most typical structure is securitization, which provides a means of increasing the supply of highly creditworthy bonds on domestic financial markets.[4] Securitization involves structuring and packaging a pool of cash flow–generating underlying assets (receivables, mortgage loans, futures revenues) into marketable securities, which are then sold to investors. Typically, a special purpose vehicle is created to purchase the assets and issue the bonds. Investors who purchase the bonds issued by the special-purpose vehicle rely on the credit quality of the future cash flow of the assets—not on the credit quality of the initial owner and seller. (Appendix 1 provides a detailed description of securitization.) Securitization helps to overcome incomplete markets, spread risk across actors (originators, credit enhancers, institutional investors), and channel financing despite an imperfect lending environment (figure ES.1).

In creating structured instruments for Latin American countries, it is important to understand the financial context—there are typically no hedge funds, no sophisticated mutual funds, no junk bond investors. Structured bond ownership will be concentrated in the hands of a few investors—AFPs and annuity providers—looking for highly creditworthy securities. Securitization through tranching structures will generally not work, since there are no potential investors for junior tranches. The originator would need to retain the junior tranche, which reduces the benefit of securitization, and a more robust set of credit enhancements could be needed to bring the bond issue to high creditworthiness.

Structured financing can help pool different underlying originators to reach a critical size and to use credit enhancements (if needed) to reach higher risk ratings. The size of multi-originator structures can meet investor needs, and such structures spread the fixed transaction costs associated with bond issuance across the pool of originators. Thriving primary markets for securitizable assets or flows are prerequisites. The originators of the pool of mortgages, leases, loans, or receivables to be securitized will generally be banks (or corporations for receivable flows) but also some nonbank financial institutions (leasing, factoring, finance companies). Less regulated independent operators (and corporations) can also prompt innovation (also because they do not take deposits) and complement incomplete credit markets. Mexican finance companies dedicated to residential mortgages (*sociedades financieras de objeto limitado* [SOFOLs]), for example, have issued several securitizations, including inflation-

Figure ES.1. A Typical Asset Securitization Transaction

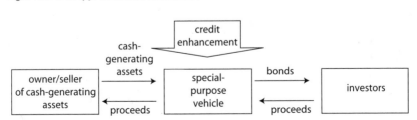

indexed bonds. Bank-related or independent originators would thereafter need to bundle the portfolio of smaller exposures and sell them off—for various reasons including gaining capital relief—issuing higher creditworthiness paper, and allowing pension funds to diversify sectorally. Because securitization reduces the direct exposure to financial intermediaries' credit risk, it will arguably not use up the exposure limit for the financial sector.[5]

For infrastructure projects or top-tier local corporations with low creditworthiness, the obstacle is less the size of debt issuance than the need for enhancing credit and capturing creditworthy future flows. Banks already use escrow accounts and different types of guarantees extensively in their financing. The goal is to replicate the approach while issuing structured bonds as a complementary source of financing to bank debt. Many potential domestic issuers are in the nontradables sector, so they would typically have better repayment capacity with local currency funding[6] and even with inflation-indexed local currency debt in some sectors (for infrastructure projects such as utilities). Institutional investors (AFPs and annuity providers) can thus respond to these needs while meeting their own investment preferences.

There are several prerequisites for structured financing to work. To make structured finance work, careful regulation is needed to ensure consistency across the different relevant laws and regulations. Primary markets and securitization need to be promoted in the context of "symbiotic finance" (Vittas 2000)—the simultaneous presence of several important elements of a modern financial system, from banks and other originating financial institutions to institutional investors, various types of securities markets, and the legal, settlement, and information systems that support modern financial systems. The legal, tax, and regulatory framework should allow for the setup of (fiscally neutral) special-purpose pass-through vehicles and for adequate treatment of credit enhancement mechanisms. True sales and the possibility of transferring credit rights are needed. For instance, for a long time in Chile, residential mortgages were the only allowed asset class for securitization, preventing the development of other classes of asset-backed securitizations.

Structured financing is no panacea but should be seen as an additional means of increasing the investment options of AFPs (and annuity providers) and of deepening financial markets. Raising structured financing is typically costly, so it must be of a critical size to absorb the structuring costs. In addition, new financial products always require frameworks—infrastructure, institutional capacity, marketing, and education—which tend to be public goods in nature. The structured securities issued tend to have very limited secondary market liquidity, as they are generally highly tailored and one-off issues, as opposed to the corporate bonds of a single issuer. The consequences of illiquidity and the need to derive sound mark-to-market procedures are not trivial. To the extent that many securitizations are issued as AAA and assuming that they retain that rating until maturity, the presence of a regular and reliable government debt program and of other structured issues of similar credit rating can help with the benchmark AAA local curve. Promoting structured financing does not replace the need to continue the long-term work on legal and institutional frameworks for stronger creditor rights and enforcement. In addition, efforts should continue on developing equity instruments (public listing, private equity) and improving the legal and institutional infrastructure for thriving credit origination. Finally, efforts should also continue to allow AFPs to invest more abroad—to optimize their portfolio allocation.

Securitization is already happening in Latin American countries that have promoted an adequate framework. A robust and growing primary market is essential. Governments—from local authorities to bilateral and multilateral entities—can play a crucial role by establishing an enabling environment and helping to start up the market.

Specific Issues per Sector and Type of Underlying Assets Are Examined in Detail in Each Chapter

Chapter 1 focuses on private pension fund investment management and the role of structured bonds. It examines the driving factors behind the varying sizes of AFPs in the region and the need to seek greater investment opportunities. It identifies some of the determinants of asset allocation by AFPs and compares expected and actual portfolio allocations. The comparison highlights that pension funds in Latin American countries seem to be overinvested locally, exposed largely to government risk, and underinvested in equity. This allocation is explained both by the set of dynamic quantitative investment limits by asset class and by complex sets of regulations that influence AFP incentives for optimizing portfolio returns.

Having a fast-growing class of investors responding to a complex set of regulations, incentives, and constraints suggests a sizable potential for the further development of structured finance instruments. Structured financing has emerged in the Latin American countries in the last couple of years, and the trend should continue and strengthen over the coming years. Some assets are easier to securitize than others, and efforts can start with these.

Chapter 2 focuses on the increasing use of structured finance for housing in Latin American countries. Most Latin American countries have severe housing shortages, both quantitatively and qualitatively. An estimated 4.2 million households in Mexico, 1.2 million households in Peru, and 50 million individuals in Brazil live in inadequate conditions. High levels of poverty, inefficient primary real estate markets, and inadequate real estate financing have resulted in the growth of shantytowns. In many Latin American countries, mortgage financing reaches only households in the top fifth of the population, although moderate- and low-income households could afford a mortgage, given longer maturities and relatively low interest rates. Several countries have increased the flow of funds to the housing sector through investment instruments such as mortgage bonds that are bought by insurers and pension funds.

As primary mortgage markets developed, countries started to move toward the securitization of outstanding mortgages to tap contractual savings funds for housing finance. This chapter describes the experience of Chile, Colombia, and Mexico in issuing mortgage-backed securities and the legal and regulatory conditions underlying the development of mortgage capital markets in these countries. Prerequisites for structured financing in the residential housing segment include the existence of sound primary markets, because the quality of a mortgage-related security depends on the quality of the pool of individual loans. Also important is standardization of lending documents and underwriting practices and professional standards of property appraisal. Important legal and regulatory prerequisites include the enforceability of mortgage pledges, adequate tax treatment of mortgage securities for both issuers and investors, and adequate protection of investors against bankruptcy of mortgage security originators or servicers. This chapter discusses the important role that governments have in fostering the appropriate legal and regulatory conditions for the development of mortgage-backed securities.

Chapter 3 deals with the less developed yet promising area of structured bonds for infrastructure financing. Infrastructure investment needs in Latin American countries over 2005–10 are projected to reach US$71 billion per year to meet the needs of current and growing populations, repair and rehabilitation, and compliance with environmental standards. Many of these investments will originate with subnational entities. Until the late 1980s, governments had been the main source of infrastructure financing. In the 1990s, as governments abandoned public provision of infrastructure due to competing demands on fiscal resources, private investment in infrastructure increased substantially. By the end of the 1990s, however, private investors had lost their appetite for infrastructure projects because of greater macroeconomic instability, growing public discontent over privatizations, and investor concerns over the regulatory and contractual framework. More recently, many infrastructure investments are brought to the private sector as concessions and financed though project finance arrangements with some credit enhancement, such as government or third-party guarantees. However, these are usually insufficient to enable infrastructure projects to raise money in capital markets, due to the high inherent risks of such projects, particularly during the construction phase.

Structured bonds for infrastructure financing can play an important role in funding selected, sound, well-structured projects that have adequate risk sharing and that provide sufficient security to institutional investors, although capital markets are not likely to become major sources of infrastructure financing in emerging economies. Some methods aim at reducing project risk, such as the use of local currency financing in loans from international lenders or of contingent liquidity facilities linked to exchange rate movements. Other methods aim at limiting the exposure of lenders to project risks, such as private bond insurance, partial credit guarantees, and securitization structures that rely on the creditworthiness of the project's flows. Domestic securitizations of future flows in 2005 in Latin American countries are estimated at US$2.7 billion, mostly for utilities and energy companies and primarily purchased by domestic pension funds. Although structured bonds are being used mostly to finance expansion and improvement of existing infrastructure projects, in the future they may be increasingly used for greenfield projects and concessions if accompanied by adequate risk enhancements.

Chapter 4 focuses on the use of structured bonds for SME finance, still in the experimental stage. SMEs account for more than 24 percent of employment and 30 percent of production in many Latin American countries, but they face difficulties in obtaining finance. Their main sources of financing are owner equity, reinvested profits, and trade credit from suppliers. Bank credit is unavailable or expensive because of perceived high credit risk, lack of qualifying collateral, and high administrative costs per dollar lent. Access to capital markets is also limited due to high issuing costs for the volume needed and because SME issues would not achieve credit ratings that would appeal to institutional investors.

The issuing of structured bonds backed by the enterprise-related assets of SMEs can be increased through the use of multi-originator securitization. In Brazil and Mexico (and starting in Peru and Argentina), the issuance of structured bonds backed by enterprise-related assets, particularly accounts receivable, is growing (although the volumes are still modest compared with those of mortgage-backed securities). The structured bonds issued to finance SMEs can achieve the needed high ratings within local markets—ratings well above those of the originator. But securitization requires a vast pool of cash flow–generating assets, which rarely exist in SMEs in most Latin American countries. This limitation can be overcome through multi-originator securitizations, which pool multiple originators into one securitization, and revolving securitizations, which replace matured receivables with similar ones on a revolving basis.

Financing for SMEs can be increased through the securitization of leasing and factoring contracts and of commercial loans. SMEs may not be able to access financing through securitization because of scale requirements and cost, but factoring and leasing firms can securitize their portfolios to boost the creditworthiness of their bond issuances and make them more appealing to institutional investors. Such securitization is relatively new in Latin American countries, but interest is likely to grow. Securitization of commercial loans to SMEs (known as collateralized loan obligations), common in other regions, is rare in Latin America and the Caribbean, where banks' portfolios of SME loans are small. In Latin American countries, this type of securitization can be originated primarily by nonbank financial intermediaries. For small banks and nonbank financial intermediaries, the major benefits of such loan portfolio securitization are access to funding and reduced financing costs; for larger banks, the main benefit is capital relief. The report discusses the role of the government in supporting small and medium loan securitizations through partial guarantees (as in Spain) to share the risk of borrower default and through the development of an SME securitization conduit (as in Germany).

Governments can catalyze the development of structured finance instruments to channel pension fund resources to underserved segments. Governments, regulators, and professional associations can provide standards for sound primary market practices to ensure the high quality of the pool of assets backing the securities sold to investors. For example, for mortgages this includes establishing professional standards of property appraisal, accurate registration and transfer of titles, sound loan origination and documentation standards, and short foreclosure processes. For loans to SMEs, standards should be set for consistent credit origination and collection procedures, transparent and accurate information on asset performance, and rapid execution of guarantees. In establishing the legal and regulatory conditions for securitization, governments and regulatory authorities need to set clear and adequate taxation and accounting rules for asset-backed securities for both issuers and investors that reflect international best practices. The legal provisions that protect bondholders against the bankruptcy of the originator or servicer must be credible. Governments can also support structured financing for infrastructure by setting up dedicated structures, including infrastructure funds, liquidity facilities, credit lines, and well-designed guarantee facilities. Similarly, governments can facilitate securitization of SME loans through well-designed and priced partial credit guarantees at the level of the overall credit portfolio, to add comfort for institutional investors. Governments can support the development of securitization infrastructure by helping with setup and transaction costs for participants. Finally, governments should ease investment rules for pension funds and insurance companies, to allow them to invest in good-quality structured securities.

Notes

1. Initially in Mexico, 65 percent of fund assets had to be held in government debt. This was later relaxed. Bolivian pension funds are still required to put a substantial percentage of their investments in public debt.

2. AFPs tend to have few high-level investment officers. Rather, their regulatory, financial, and competitive incentives favor investments in back-office and marketing staffing.

3. Except if there are massive transfers of pension fund affiliates between AFPs, in which case they could arrange to shift securities instead of cash, if the framework allows it.

4. As structured financing develops, there will be a greater role for derivatives to permit enhanced tailoring and risk management. Derivatives can help bridge slightly differing investor and issuer needs (such as fixed and floating interest rates or currency mismatches). The first generation will be securitization bonds, but a second generation could be synthetic securitization through credit derivatives.

5. In securitizations, some exposure to the financial intermediary's operational risk (as the servicer of the loans) remains, but it is mitigated through back-up servicer and credit enhancements.

6. Except in totally dollarized economies, or if local currency financing is prohibitive even after adjusting for the devaluation risk of dollar-denominated debt.

References

de la Torre, Augusto, and Sergio L. Schmukler. 2004. "Whither Latin American Capital Markets?" Latin America and Caribbean Regional Study, World Bank, Washington, DC.

de la Torre, Augusto, Juan Carlos Gozzi, and Sergio L. Schmukler. 2006. "Financial Development in Latin America: Big Emerging Issues, Limited Policy Answers." Policy Research Working Paper 3963, World Bank, Washington, DC.

Vittas, Dimitri. 2000. "Pension Reform and Capital Market Development: 'Feasibility' and 'Impact' Preconditions." Policy Research Working Paper 2414, World Bank, Washington, DC.

Abbreviations

AFPs	*administradoras de fondos de pensión* (private pension funds)
AIOS	International Association of Latin American Pension Funds Supervisors
Arg$	Argentine peso
ARS	average return of the system
BOT	build-own-transfer
CBs	*certificados bursátiles* (securities certificates)
FIDC	*fundo de investimento en dereitos creditorios* (receivables investment fund)
FTPYME	Fondo de Titulización de Activos Pyme
GDP	gross domestic product
IDB	Interamerican Development Bank
IFC	International Finance Corporation
KfW	Kreditantstalt für Wiederaufbau
Mex$	Mexican peso
MFIs	microfinance institutions
Nafin	Nacional Financiera

NBFI	nonbank financial institution
OPIC	Overseas Private Investment Corporation
PROMISE	Programme for Mittelstand-loan Securitization
R$	Brazilian *real*
SBA	Small Business Administration
SFN	Servicios Financieros Navistar
SMEs	small and medium enterprises
SOFOLs	*sociedades financieras de objeto limitado* (nonbank finance companies)
US$	U.S. dollar
UTE	Administración Nacional de Usinas y Transmisiones Eléctricas

Investment Management of Defined Contribution Pension Funds and the Role of Structured Bonds

This chapter examines the potential drivers of growth in assets under management in private pension funds (*administradoras de fondos de pensión*, or AFPs) in Latin America. Actual growth will depend on how these factors play out in each country. The chapter looks first at good practice in asset management by private pension funds worldwide and then compares it with actual asset allocation Latin American AFPs. Actual practice is shaped in large measure by regulations in each country. The chapter offers some avenues to explore for countries seeking to fine tune their current regulations to bring them closer to good practice internationally, given regulators' priorities and objectives. Finally, the chapter argues that the overall context of regulations and domestic realities in capital market development has created momentum for structured bonds that appears permanent and growing.

The Issues

Several Latin American countries have embarked on extensive pension reforms, introducing fully funded private pension system pillars, but years later many expectations remain unfulfilled. This chapter focuses on investment management issues. While defined contribution pension systems face structural issues and challenges for increasing population coverage, reducing costs, and promoting competition, these concerns are not addressed in this chapter, though they are touched on to the extent that they have an impact on the growth rates and the portfolio management decisions of AFPs.

Regulators have a very delicate task in regulating AFPs to strike a balance between preserving workers' savings and optimizing wage replacement rates. Fully funded pension systems should help to achieve two challenging objectives: to reach the highest possible replacement rate (the ratio of pensions to the worker's final wage) and to limit the volatility in replacement rates across cohorts. The challenge is to realize high investment returns over the working life of workers while maintaining investment behavior consistent with the prudent investor model.

Returns to workers on pension savings can benefit substantially from some diversification away from public debt. Pension fund assets have been invested largely in public debt. If local capital markets could offer multiple high-quality investment opportunities, pension funds would be able to diversify portfolios and achieve yields superior to those on public debt. This requires aligning the incentives of pension fund managers with the objective of maximizing affiliates' (workers') savings. For example, since AFP managers are pure asset managers, they may not look systematically for long-duration assets, even though workers' savings under their management are long term. Finally, a sound regulatory framework should accompany greater asset diversification while protecting the interests of workers.

AFPs can be allowed flexibility in degree of liquidity and maturity of securities, but not so much in creditworthiness. Unlike some investors, AFP affiliates do not necessarily require a high level of liquidity of securities so long as an effective valuation methodology can be derived. AFPs have proven to be "buy and hold" investors, due partly to the funds' fast asset growth, which is projected to continue. There are two major requirements for securities to be considered worthy of investment: a high level of creditworthiness and a size large enough to make these instruments appealing to fund managers.[1] This means that a limited number of domestic issuers can easily meet the institutional investors' criteria.

As the defined contribution system matures into its payout phase, life insurance companies will also grow into an important class of institutional investors. As affiliates of the defined contribution system reach retirement age, they will need to buy annuities, and life insurance companies, as annuity providers, will also seek high-quality, long-term domestic securities.

Structured finance transactions can help to bridge the gap between institutional investors' needs and potential issuers. Securitization and other types of engineered bonds provide the market with highly rated private debt whose credit quality does not depend on that of the issuer, but on a set of segregated assets and guarantees whose proceeds ensure future debt repayment. Structured finance transactions include the securitization of assets such as commercial and housing loans, trade receivables or leasing contracts, and expected cash flows from infrastructure project finance.

This chapter has three main sections. It identifies the drivers of private pension fund growth in Latin American countries. It then discusses the composition of AFP portfolios and their main determinants, including investment limits and regulatory factors that indirectly affect investment decisions. The chapter concludes with a discussion of the potential scope for structured securities to help AFPs find new high-quality issuances and diversify their portfolios.

What Determines Pension Fund Growth in Latin America?

Mandatory private pension funds in the 10 Latin American countries that have undergone pension reform have doubled over the past three years. Private pension funds in Latin America have been growing at an average annual rate of 30 percent, and assets under management in these funds totaled US$186 billion at the end of 2005 (close to US$318 billion including Brazil). These funds become important as institutional investors, holding assets representing almost 14 percent of the combined GDP of reforming countries—and as much as 60 percent in Chile (figure 1.1).

The accumulated funds do not represent a net increase in internal savings in the countries, but rather a shift in resources from the general government budget to the private sector asset management industry. All else being equal, funds in AFPs would be equivalent to the incremental cash deficit of the public defined benefit scheme. Generally, however, pension reforms were accompanied by reforms of the public defined benefit scheme and by attempts to limit the immediate impact on the deficit. Only Chile passed significant tax reforms to compensate for this. In the other countries the residual deficit is largely debt financed, which explains why private pension funds hold largely public debt.

The gradual but steady accumulation of contractual savings implies that the longer a system is in operation, the larger the volume of assets accumulated. However, other factors in the design and implementation of

Figure 1.1. Year of Reform and Size of Mandatory Defined-Contribution Pension Pillar in Latin American Countries, 2005

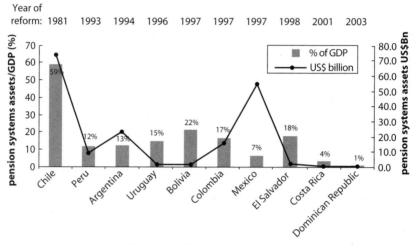

Source: Internacional Association of Latin American Pension Funds Supervisors Statistical Bulletin No. 12.

Note: Year of reform refers to the year when pension funds started operations. Data for Mexico exclude balances with Infonavit, a public housing finance entity collecting mandatory pension-like savings.

the pension reform can influence the overall size of the defined contribution system. Assets tend to accumulate more slowly in the fully funded pillar when the transition is longer or where there is a residual pay-as-you-go pillar. For example, growth is slower in countries that have allowed workers to switch between unfunded public and funded private pillars, as in Colombia and Mexico,[2] or that have allowed new workers to opt into an unfunded public pillar, as in Argentina and Peru. Knowing which reform design is superior in meeting the long-term interests of workers is important but beyond the scope of this report.

Growth of pension funds is affected by structural factors related to rate of contributions and effective coverage of the system. The rate of long-term capital accumulation in individual accounts, also called the contribution rate (measured as a percentage of the salary of affiliates) affects pension system size. Similarly, the rate of accumulation of assets is influenced by the level of effective coverage of the economically active population.[3] Effective coverage in Latin America is quite low, disappointing the expectations of supporters of pension reform (figure 1.2). Coverage is a complex issue, about which much has been written. It is affected by the size of the informal economy, the density of contributions—typically low in Latin America, despite costly follow-ups to get employers to contribute on behalf of their workers—and such design choices as maintenance of a defined benefit pillar.[4]

The real rate of investment returns is also a driver of accumulated assets under management. The real rate of gross investment returns has been positive and relatively high in all reforming countries in Latin America (figure 1.3).[5] For the most part returns reflect the high level of real interest rates in most Latin American countries a few years ago, the result of rigorous anti-inflationary and stabilization policies. More recently, especially in countries where stabilization policies have been successful, real interest rates have gradually declined, giving rise to substantial capital gains that prolonged high real returns for AFPs holding long-term fixed-rate bonds. Returns across AFPs within a given country appear to be fairly homogeneous, due largely to the similar composition of their investment portfolios and their high concentration in public debt.

In most countries the ability of pension funds to generate high real returns is being exhausted, as evidenced by lower yields in 2005. With the exception of Colombia and Peru, which witnessed exceptional stock market appreciation, real returns achieved by AFPs in 2005 are well below historical levels (figure 1.2). Asset accumulation through returns on

Figure 1.2. Mandatory Defined-Contribution Pillar Effective Coverage, 2005

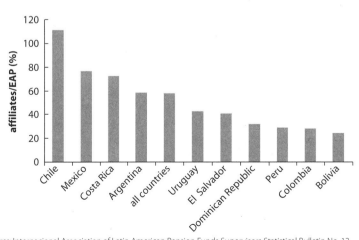

Source: Internacional Association of Latin American Pension Funds Supervisors Statistical Bulletin No. 13.

EAP is economically active population.

Figure 1.3. Gross Real Returns on Investment, Historical and Last 12 Months

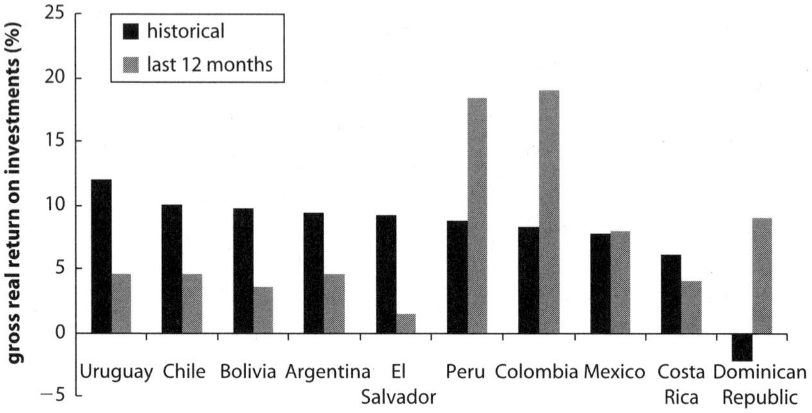

Source: Internacional Association of Latin American Pension Funds Supervisors Statistical Bulletin No. 12.

investments will depend largely on private pension funds' ability to diversify into a wider variety of investment instruments, both domestic and foreign. However, local markets lack the financial depth to provide alternatives to public debt securities, and many governments have been reluctant to allow pension funds to invest in foreign securities.

As the system matures into the payout phase, a full picture of defined contribution pension systems will include a growing role for annuity providers. Typically, pensioners who choose to receive their pension as an annuity will be serviced by life insurance companies. In Chile, when the annuity-related assets of life insurance companies are added to the defined contribution pension system, the total exceeds 80 percent of GDP. More recently reforming countries have yet to see growth in annuities.

What Determines Pension Fund Asset Allocation?

This section examines some of the challenges in pension portfolio allocation, the regulations that influence it, and the complex interplay of regulations over time. There is an extensive yet still evolving literature on management of defined contribution mandatory pension fund investment, on the preferred asset allocation approach, and on the role of the regulator in influencing such allocation.

The regulator has to set rules to ensure that AFPs act in the best interests of their clients. AFPs are managing the main source of income after retirement of workers who are generally not knowledgeable enough to influence AFP investments. As such, the literature has moved toward recommending a regulatory framework in line with the prudent investor rule to settle the principal-agent problem.[6]

Optimizing Asset Allocation of Defined Contribution Pension Funds— A Difficult Undertaking

This section summarizes lessons learned from international experience and the evolving literature on asset management by private pension funds. The discussion starts by highlighting some of the complex choices that private pension funds face to determine optimal asset allocation. The theoretical literature suffers from many shortcomings because of the need to make many assumptions that are fundamentally implausible or not applicable to all workers. The following section analyzes the actual portfolios of AFPs in Latin America.

What constitutes an optimal risk-adjusted return, and what is the optimal level of risk for a defined contribution mandatory pension fund? Rational workers (and private pension funds on their behalf) should seek to maximize their expected pension, under the constraint that since this future flow is crucial to preserve them from poverty in old age, it should be invested relatively conservatively and so should have a lower level of risk than voluntary savings portfolios. The funds being accumulated will typically be retrieved only in the very long term, which should allow for more flexibility in investment management, and the optimization exercise should take this time horizon into account. The recent literature argues that defined contribution pension fund managers should seek to optimize two parameters: to maximize retiring workers' replacement rate, which includes minimizing the annuity rate risk,[7] and—a less obvious objective—to reduce the volatility of the replacement rate across cohorts, for individuals with the same contribution and salary history. This is challenging as, by construction, defined contribution schemes, with individual accounts, minimize solidarity or cross-subsidization across cohorts.

An important issue is defining the optimal combination of equity and fixed-income investments. Conventional wisdom calls for decreasing equity holdings with increasing age, but the recent literature questions this interpretation of life-cycle investment. Shiller (2005) runs several simulations for the U.S. market and concludes that the general rule of thumb of holding a percentage of stocks equal to 100 minus the age of the worker is not necessarily optimal, as it understates the desirable share of equity investments in older age. In addition, some researchers (Viceira 2001) argue that young workers should leverage up to invest more than 100 percent of their savings in equity, to account for the fact that their human capital is the larger part of their wealth. At the opposite end of the spectrum, others (Benzoni and others 2004) maintain that young workers should invest only about 20 percent in stocks, assigning a rising weight to equities as they age, to account for the positive correlation between labor income and stock returns. Bodie (2005a) adds that workers with relatively riskier human capital should invest relatively less in equity, all else being equal.[8] Many Latin American countries have a high level of informality or uncertainty in employment outlook and workforces that experience frequent interruptions in employment history, suggesting that the argument about the riskiness of human capital may be quite relevant. So, most of the literature shows that a portfolio without any equity exposure is never optimal and that some tailoring is required in asset allocation over the life cycle of the worker, although there is no general agreement on the shape of such tailoring.

Most of the literature considers only the accumulation phase in evaluating the performance of portfolio allocation, ignoring the importance of annuity rate risk upon retirement. Recent work highlights that life-cycle finance should span the whole expected life of the worker, including the payout phase (Bodie 2005b). And if the expected action upon retirement is to buy an inflation-indexed annuity, then annuity rate risk might be minimized by reaching the retirement age with an individual account that replicates an indexed annuity in its portfolio allocation (see box 1.1 on annuity providers' asset management). At this stage, it is too early to have a definitive view on the annuitization decision in defined contribution pension systems and the definition of life-cycle investments.

The optimal domestic portfolio for pension investment depends on the long-term historical price-return data of traded securities, information that is typically unavailable in Latin American markets. These data are needed to derive historical correlations, volatilities, and risk premia per class of assets and per sector, among others. While past performance does not necessarily predict future performance, it is a necessary starting point and essential to calibrate any projection model. The absence of well-established domestic capital markets makes it harder for Latin American AFPs to decide on optimal asset allocation. Efforts to develop databases of historical prices of financial assets should be encouraged. Until such data become available, data from international capital markets can be used as a proxy to estimate expected real returns and risk levels for various types of assets and sectors.

International investments appear to be a straightforward solution for increasing returns at a given level of risk, but they are a sensitive issue for

Box 1.1

Annuity providers' investment management

In the payout phase, retirees can either buy an annuity, typically from a life insurer, receiving a constant amount per year, usually inflation-adjusted, or opt for a phased withdrawal, with no assurance that it will last for their remaining life, possibly serviced by the same AFP that managed the accumulation phase of their account. Annuity providers have a liability that depends on actual residual life of the retiree, so their investment decisions will seek to ensure returns that at least meet their liabilities while also generating profits. The "riskless" investment strategy would be to buy inflation-indexed fixed-income instruments that match the expected (uncertain) duration of the annuity liability.

However, in a competitive environment the annuity provider will seek the best portfolio to support a good annuity, sustainable in real terms, with an optimal distribution rate—per year of the initial capital—also called the money's worth ratio. According to extensive simulations (Fidelity 2005), such a portfolio should always include a combination of stocks and bonds, with the actual ratio depending on the country-specific risk premium, volatility, and correlation across classes of assets.

policymakers. Investing in the financial markets of other economies typically lowers the risk for the same level of return, given imperfect correlations of risks across financial markets. In addition, this enables investors to tap into a much larger pool of financial assets, solving the problem of low domestic supply of good investments. For instance, Latin American equity and sovereign debt markets represent less than 1 percent of the world's financial markets. Yet pension savings allocation in Latin American countries typically underuses such global diversification opportunities, as explained later.

A related asset allocation decision concerns the optimal exposure to foreign exchange risk in pension portfolio allocation. There is debate on whether AFPs should have to hedge foreign exchange exposures. Having other currencies in the portfolio offers the benefit of diversification away from exposure to local currency, from a pure asset management perspective. Also, the cost of hedging can be prohibitive in largely inefficient forward markets, where bid-offer spreads tend to be high and forward rates are typically very poor predictors of future foreign exchange rates. An additional issue is deciding on the tenor of the hedge if the international investment is a strategic, long-term stake. Moreover, there is some evidence that foreign currency value serves as a partial hedge to volatility in an international portfolio (Walker 2006). Finally, in highly dollarized economies, it is controversial to impose a local currency denomination on mandatory pension savings, which could be quite costly to pensioners by lowering their income.

While the funds under management in AFPs are long term in nature, AFPs are pure asset managers. As such, they may not systematically look for long maturities and durations in their investments. The strategic asset allocation may be to seek a majority of longer-term securities, but tactical realignments related to opportunistic decisions about market shifts may lead to temporary preferences for mostly short-term securities. Moreover, some regulations, such as daily mark-to-market requirements, may lead to a preference for securities with low short-term volatility, which is typically high for longer-duration instruments.

For specific asset classes, evidence diverges on whether an active investment management style leads to higher net yields than a passive investment strategy, such as exchange-traded funds-replicating indexes. Some back-testing work finds that actively managed funds underperform the benchmark index, and more so when factoring in the higher fees of actively managed funds compared with funds that replicate an index. That said, index replication is not as easy to achieve in small emerging markets as in large markets, which reduces its efficiency.

Because of the complexity of pension portfolio optimization decisions, it is important that AFPs have advanced decision-making tools and highly qualified staff. This means having strong management information systems and decision-making tools; formulating an annual investment strategy, with monthly updates; fixing internal limits per factor of risk and group of factors; setting benchmarks; monitoring the tracking error against the benchmark; tracking client population characteristics; developing a combination of active (tactical) and passive (strategic) asset management; having good projections and scenarios of cash flows and of market variable modeling capabilities; seeking balance between absolute return optimization for workers and relative return (compared with peers or benchmarks); and tracking the costs and benefits of a sophisticated investment management unit. Finally, use of derivatives allows more flexibility in investment management (for example, if issuers prefer fixed-rate bonds and the AFPs prefer indexed, a swap can reconcile both) but increases the need for advanced systems, middle- and back-office support, and smart, risk-based supervision.

Actual Asset Allocation of Defined Contribution Pension Funds

Preliminary efficient frontier analysis in several countries points to subop-timal AFP portfolio allocation in Latin America. This section takes a look at the actual portfolio composition, keeping in mind that methodologies need to be improved.[9]

A snapshot of Latin American AFP asset allocation by class of assets as of the end of 2005 shows a high concentration of public debt within AFP investment portfolios, especially in recently reformed systems. At the end of 2005, public debt accounted for almost half the total assets under man-agement by private pension funds in Latin America (figure 1.4). The con-centration of public debt within AFP portfolios varies significantly across countries, but it is highest among countries that have recently undergone pension reform. This may indicate that regulators tend to impose stricter rules on asset classes in which AFPs can invest when the system is new and there is no domestic track record in fund management.

The high concentration in public debt among recently reformed pen-sion systems is also explained in part by the reform-financing mechanism. The shift to defined contribution systems implies larger cash deficits in the public pay-as-you-go system, which is typically debt financed by the government. In such cases, whether directly through transition regulations or indirectly through the sheer volume of issues, the new private pension fund industries have been called on to fund government securities. This has helped governments obtain the liquidity to fund such transition gaps while providing pension fund managers with a relatively safe investment. However, these transition-financing arrangements are probably subopti-mal from an asset allocation perspective.

In markets where AFPs have accumulated large funds (Chile, for exam-ple), they have grown into a significant public debt holder. This may indi-cate that they have exhausted the available possibilities for private securities (figure 1.5).

Attractive historical yields underpin the strong appetite of institutional investors for government securities. Government debt has historically provided high yields in many Latin American countries. As macroeco-nomic stability and low inflation environments translate into low interest rates, the search for yield may push AFPs to seek alternative investments.

In contrast, AFP investments in private sector securities are modest. The factors encouraging investment in public securities may have led to the crowding out of private securities, limiting appetites and opportuni-ties for seeking optimal asset allocation. In addition, most private assets are issued by financial institutions and include both bank bonds and, to a

Figure 1.4. Asset Allocation of Pension Fund Assets, December 2005

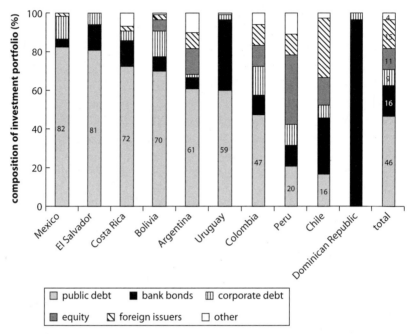

Source: Internacional Association of Latin American Pension Funds Supervisors Statistical Bulletin No. 14.

Figure 1.5. Participation of Pension Funds in Total Government Debt

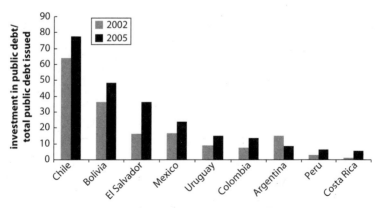

Source: Authors' calculations based on data from the Internacional Association of Latin American Pension Funds Supervisors.

lesser extent, structured finance bonds.[10] Corporate debt represents less than 1/10 of AFP assets and is usually issued by the largest and highest rated corporates, since smaller issuers are deterred from entering the market by the high cost of issuance. Investments in equity are much lower than would be expected (11 percent on average), and investments in foreign assets are modest in most countries. While the average size of international investments by defined benefit pension plans is between 25 percent and 30 percent in many high-income countries, it averages 15 percent in Latin America, and varies between zero (Mexico, the Dominican Republic, Uruguay) and more than 25 percent (Chile).

The Influence of Regulatory Investment Limits
This pattern of AFP asset allocation is determined in part by the regulations governing AFPs. The impacts of these regulations sometimes conflict and often diverge from good practice. In fine-tuning the current regulations to more closely approximate international good practice, however, regulators need to consider their own priorities and objectives.

Broadly speaking, countries either follow the prudent investor rule or apply a strategy of quantitative investment limits. The prudent investor rule is simple: pension funds should manage their portfolios as a prudent investor would, which in the Anglo-Saxon world implies proper portfolio diversification. A quantitative investment regime involves direct restrictions on the portfolio by both instrument and issuer. Operation of a pension system on a prudent investor rule requires an efficient court system with well-trained and informed judges, capable of establishing clear jurisprudence on prudent investor behavior and of guaranteeing its swift enforcement for market participants. This is typically not the case in most emerging market economies, and thus countries have typically turned to quantitative investment limits.

The complexity of quantitative investment limits varies across countries. One problem with developing an investment limits model is the lack of a framework to justify the levels of risks associated with its parameters when complexity is high. Chile has a very complex set of limits. As the capital market develops, the problems become more evident. Authorities are starting to consider a model of risk-based supervision (discussed briefly later in the chapter).

In reforming Latin American countries, the investment regime for pension funds involves maximum exposure limits by instruments, individual issuers, and issuance, which vary by country and over time. In several cases, these limits have turned into binding constraints (for example, in

Mexico, only recently and with rigid limitations are AFPs allowed to invest in equities; in Peru, only recently are they allowed to invest more than 10 percent abroad; in Colombia, they are not allowed to invest more than 50 percent in public debt). In countries where investment regulations are set at a very detailed level in the law (for example, Chile), there is little flexibility to relax and adjust based on market evolution. In countries where investment regulations are set through regulatory institutions (by the pensions superintendent or central bank, for example), more flexibility is possible. Table 1.1 provides a snapshot of some key asset class limits in Latin American countries at one point in time.

Fund managers' investment decisions are heavily influenced by the investment limits and asset allocation rules imposed by regulators. Since AFPs' assets are mandatory retirement contributions by workers, governments have sought to protect these savings by imposing minimum levels of creditworthiness for allowable investments. Rules are based on independent assessments by rating agencies and usually confine the universe of qualifying securities to those with an investment-grade rating[11] on the local scale.[12] However, while security is justifiably paramount, investment rules can lead to excessive risk aversion and avoidance of investments in some qualifying securities. For example, in some countries, rigid investment rules require AFPs to promptly dispose of any assets whose rating falls below the designated minimum. In the absence of an active secondary market for subinvestment-grade assets, forced liquidations would generate significant losses. Accordingly, AFPs have protected themselves against the risk of securities downgrades by investing only in securities whose ratings are well above the minimum requirement, further constraining the universe of de facto qualifying securities.[13]

Other investment rules further limit the universe of qualifying securities. Investment rules in many countries include limits on the concentration of AFP investment portfolios in public and private domestic instruments.[14] Investment rules also define limits on the participation of an AFP in a given issue, a disincentive for investment in small issues as the consequent small exposure does not justify the relatively high operating and monitoring costs. Investment in foreign securities is either barred or significantly constrained in many countries to curtail the transfer of domestic savings abroad.

As systems mature, the relaxation of restrictions on investments in specific asset classes can help AFPs diversify investments and thus provide greater stability in portfolio value, but this shift does not always happen as desired. Investment rules have resulted in relatively uniform portfolios dominated by government bonds, even though authorities have tried to create further incentives for diversification through mechanisms such as multiple funds within each AFP (see box 1.2). As quantitative limits are relaxed, this should facilitate prudent diversification and the search for high expected returns with a reasonable degree of risk. However, the impact of widening limits will continue to be constrained by the depth of local capital markets and the lag time for AFPs to shift their asset allocations and for new instruments to develop. Figure 1.6 highlights the example of Colombia, where most asset class limits do not seem to be binding, suggesting that the limitation may have more to do with the availability of domestic instruments.

The relaxation of limits on foreign assets' investments can enhance the portfolio allocation of pension funds as a complement to the domestic securities markets. Foreign assets account for an average of 15 percent of pension fund assets in Latin America. However, this figure is heavily influenced by the comparatively high share of investments in foreign assets in Chile (limited at 30 percent, the highest in the region). With the exceptions of Colombia, Peru, and Argentina, foreign assets play a negligible part in asset allocation in Latin American pension funds. While relaxing the foreign investment limit is important for optimizing the risk return on workers' savings, it is unclear how it would affect the appetite for domestic securities or what the optimal foreign investment limit is. The resistance to higher limits is usually linked to a political desire to finance the growth of the domestic economy, the perception that AFPs have local currency liabilities, and the fear that they have a limited understanding of global financial markets (home bias).

Regulators should refrain from tapping into AFP assets to direct investments toward government priority sectors in a way that jeopardizes workers' old-age savings. The accumulation of sizable long-term funds within AFPs gives governments an incentive to implement their economic agenda through directed investment limits that would steer AFPs to invest in priority sectors. If specified limits do not preserve workers' interests by adhering to a prudent investor rule, this could jeopardize workers' old-age savings, leading to higher poverty rates in old age or higher fiscal burdens for the government.

Investment regulations should take into account the level of development of each country's capital markets and the level of sophistication of AFP managers. Countries that introduced mandatory defined contribution pensions have widely varying degrees of domestic capital market development, and the expectations of active and diverse investments from AFPs should take this into account. Local financial regulators should, as

Table 1.1. Snapshot of Some Investment Limits by Asset Class in Latin American Countries with Mandatory Defined Contribution Pension Systems

	Chile: funds A, B, C, D, E	Peru: funds type 1, type 2, type 3	Argentina	Uruguay	Bolivia	Colombia	Mexico	El Salvador	Costa Rica	Dominican Republic
Noninvestment grade	A: 10%, B: 10%, C: 10%, D: 5%, E: 5%	Not regulated	n.a.	0%	Not regulated	0%	0%	0%	0%	n.a.
Multiple funds	Yes	Yes (FIAP 2007)	n.a.	n.a.	n.a.	n.a.	Yes	n.a.	n.a.	n.a.
Equity	A: 60%, B: 50%, C: 30%, D: 15%, E: 0%	Type 1: 10%, type 2: 45%, Type 3:80%	50%	25%	20%	30%	Fund I: 0%, fund II: 15% (capital-protected notes only)	Local: 20%	10%	30%
Foreign investment	30%	13.5%	10%	0%	12%	20%	20%	0%	25% (50% if justified)	0% (not regulated)
Financial institutions	A: 40%, B: 40%, C: 50%, D: 70%, E: 80%	40% (Iglesias 2004)	Local: 30%	30%	60%	30%	AAA: 100%, AA: 35%, A: 5%	40%	Local: 20%	60%
Corporate	A: 30%, B: 30%, C: 40%, D: 50%, E: 60% [a]	Type 1: 100%, type 2: 75%, type 3: 70% [b]	40%	30%	45%	30%	AAA: 100%, AA: 35%, A: 5%	Local: 40%	AAA: 70%, AA: 50%, A: 20%	70%
Government	A: 40%, B: 40%, C: 50%, D: 70%, E: 80%	government and central bank: 40%	central government: 50%, local government: 30%	60%	No limit	50%	No limit	80%	government and central bank: 50%	n.a.[e]
Asset-backed securities—Future flows securities	Yes	Yes (limit set per asset-backed security)	40%, 10%, 10%[c]	25%	30%	30%	Yes	n.a.	N.A.	70% (mortgage bonds)

Derivatives	Yes (AIOS 2004)	Type 1: 10%, type 2: 10%, type 3: 20%	0%	n.a.[d]	Allowed only for the coverage of interest rate risk, exchange rate risk, and stocks	Allowed if underlying asset allowed (forwards, future, swaps, and options) Counterparty credit risk limits, AAA-5%, AA-3%, A-1%	0%	n.a.	n.a.
Private equity funds	N.A.	Yes	N.A.	25%	5% (combined private equity funds and investment funds)	Within the limit of foreign investment	0%	n.a.	10%
Investment funds	A: 40%, B: 30%, C: 20%, D: 10%, E: 0%	15% (Iglesias 2004)	20%	25%	5% (combined private equity funds and investment funds)	0%	20%	10%	20% (Only funds for development of housing sector)

Sources: Limits on Chile, Uruguay, Bolivia, Colombia, Mexico, El Salvador, and Costa Rica based on information provided by FIAP in 2007, unless otherwise noted; limits on Argentina and Dominican Republic based on information provided by AIOS in 2007; limits on Peru based on information sent by the Superintendency of Peru in 2007, unless otherwise noted.

Note: FIAP is International Federation of Pension Funds Administrators; AIOS is International Association of Latin American Pension Funds Supervisors; n.a. = not applicable; N.A. = not available.

a. Corporate bonds of public and private firms.
b. Fixed-income limit on all bonds (sovereign and corporate).
c. Mortgage bonds 40%, Direct Investment Funds Securities 10%, Structured Trust Funds 10%.
d. Limit not defined but interpreted as 0% according to market conditions.
e. Ten percent limit for securities issued by the Banco Nacional de la Vivienda (mortgage securities development), FIAP 2007.

Figure 1.6. Example of Investment Limits and Actual Use in Colombia, December 2005

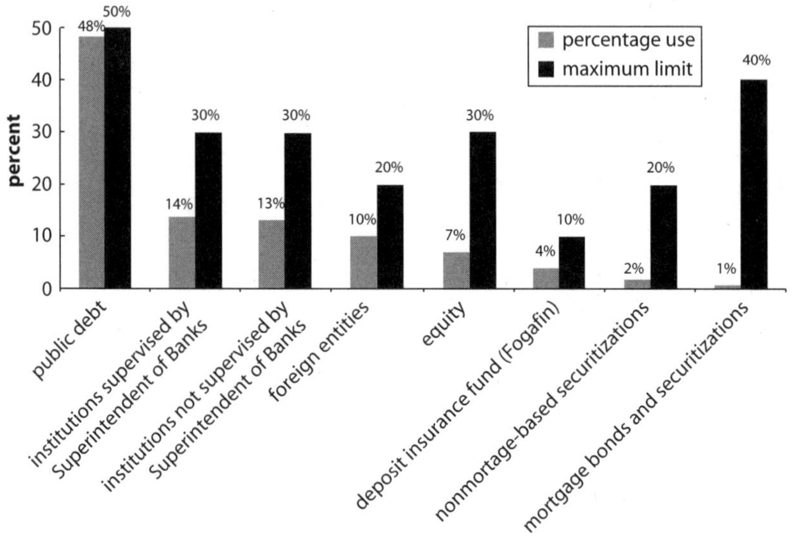

Source: Superintendencia Financiera (Rudolph and others 2006).

appropriate, promote capital market development and provide incentives for increasing the investment skills of AFP managers.

Other Regulations Affecting Incentives in Investment Management
In addition to quantitative investment limits, other regulations can have indirect impacts on investment decisions. This section examines such regulations, which are briefly outlined in table 1.2.

Minimum liquidity requirements. To ensure that AFPs are building wealth on behalf of workers, the regulator needs to insist on regular valuation of investments. The issue is whether daily valuation is needed, or whether monthly valuation could suffice. Also—in Peru, for example—regulators seem to require excessively high liquidity of instruments, imposing potentially strongly penalizing "liquidity factors" for evaluating conservatively illiquid securities. While it is important to be cautious in such situations, an overly conservative approach may prevent workers from benefiting from an "illiquidity premium" that they would gladly—and safely—tap into. Many countries have allowed for only a small percentage of investments not to be regularly marked to market (for example, private equity

Box 1.2

The Life-Cycle Multiple Funds and the Development of Securities Markets

A major problem of the single-fund system is that it is provided to all workers independently of age, income, and other characteristics. Governments should offer portfolio options to workers at different stages of the life cycle, so that workers could choose the portfolio that best meets their needs within government-established guidelines. The government should also consider dynamic default options, including automatically moving workers to less risky funds as they age. Different funds should be designed to achieve portfolio allocations that serve the long-term interests of workers. The main elements for differentiating funds should be equity holdings, maturity of assets, and eventually holdings of foreign instruments. For example, the least risky fund should have a portfolio profile similar to what an annuity provider would have, including primarily inflation-indexed, fixed-income instruments with long durations.

Countries with more mature defined contribution pension systems (Chile, Mexico, Peru) have moved or are moving (Colombia) to multiple-fund systems, allowing AFPs to offer a number of funds to suit different risk profiles. This approach is a variant of the life-cycle portfolio, which shifts the portfolio composition over the life of the worker from a higher concentration of risky equity investments into more fixed-income (preferably inflation-indexed) investments. The advent of a wider variety of risk-profiled funds permits increased diversification of investment instruments. However, it requires the existence of a reasonable variety of qualifying investment instruments in the market.

funds up to 5 percent of all assets in Chile, Peru, and Colombia). Also, privatizations are treated differently in several countries. Bonds and stocks from small issuers and securitized bonds will typically be illiquid, as will over-the-counter derivatives, so there is a need to focus on mark-to-market methodologies and tools for immunization, synthetic unwinding, or temporary liquidity (while taking into account that pension funds cannot typically be leveraged).

Minimum size of issue or issuer requirements. Regulators may err on the side of caution with size requirements, thus excluding small issuers of good quality or newcomers, a possibly redundant measure given existing

Table 1.2. Selected Regulations with a Potential Impact on Investment Decisions in Private Pension Funds

Regulation's impact on efficient portfolio allocation	Positive impacts	Negative impacts	Net impact
Minimum liquidity of instrument (compared with mark-to-market requirement)	Mitigates principal-agent risk by timely return revelation	Can cause undue focus on liquid securities, even though liquidity is not crucial for investors with a long horizon. Can cause undue focus on the short term	Positive if focus is on adequate valuation rules as opposed to the necessity of a secondary market for each security
Minimum size of issue or issuer requirement	None; redundant given requirement to obtain risk ratings	Unnecessarily excludes a large number of possibly appealing investments whose access is already limited because of size	Negative
Capital adequacy per asset risk weighting and reserve requirements	Motivates prudent investor behavior	Focus on risk minimization, while return is not optimized (for example, for equal rating, favoring government debt that has zero risk weight)	Unclear
Minimum return guarantee by AFP	Ensure minimum cumulative returns to protect workers' savings	May lead to overly conservative investment pattern	Generally negative
Value-at-risk limit	Makes supervisors more comfortable to relax quantitative limits	If limit is based on short-term horizon, may lead to inadequate investment decisions	Depends on design
Fee structure			
Minimum pension guarantee by government	Not applicable	May motivate imprudent risk taking in investments	Marginal

Source: Staff analysis based on literature, own previous work, and policy dialogue.

requirements for risk rating. For instance, besides requiring two risk ratings, the Peruvian regulator de facto requires that AFPs invest mainly in liquid instruments issued by large enterprises, as a result of minimum size of capital, minimum proven track record, and minimum liquidity requirements. Thus, in some cases, to reach new or small issuers, AFPs have to go through investment funds, mutual funds, or securitization.

Capital adequacy and reserve requirements. Risk-adjusted capital requirements favor government debt, which carries a zero risk weighting. Within each domestic market government debt is considered risk free and carries a zero risk-adjusted equity rating. To maximize their return on equity and minimize the locked-in equity amount, AFP fund managers will therefore try to invest in government debt, which carries the lowest risk weighting. This incentive will eventually be reduced as Basel 2 regulations begin coming into effect.[15]

Minimum return guarantee. Most countries require a minimum return guarantee from AFPs, which influences their investment decisions. This guarantee has usually been expressed relative to the average return of the pension industry and has been accompanied by minimum reserve requirements for AFP management. While the risk to AFP managers of losing their capital if the return guarantee is triggered may have intensified the herding behavior of pension funds, pension funds are known to be susceptible to herd behavior even where there are few or no portfolio restrictions and no minimum return guarantees. In most Latin American countries, the minimum return guarantee formula is derived exclusively from the average return of the system (table 1.3). The calculation horizon (number of months of return) is important, too. Longer tracking horizons in the minimum return guarantees (60 months in Peru compared with 12 in Argentina, for example) seem to work better as they reduce incentives to engage in excessive turnover and "short-termism."

Value-at-risk limits. There is a trend of moving toward risk-based supervision and value-at-risk limits for AFPs, especially in mature pension systems. Mexico has already implemented such supervision, and Chile, Colombia, and Peru are considering it, while already asking AFPs to regularly measure and report their value at risk. Such an approach should take into account the longer time horizon of AFP assets under management to avoid value-at-risk limits leading to short-termism. Well-formulated value-at-risk limits and risk-based supervision can lead to significant relax-

Table 1.3. Design of Minimum Return Guarantee in Selected Countries

Country	Methodology	Computation period	Evaluation
Argentina	Min (70% of ARS; ARS −2%)	12 months	Monthly
Colombia	A. 70% of ARS	36 months	Quarterly
	B . 70% of synthetic[a] portfolio		
	70% of return of stock index		
	70% of return of S&P 500		
	Minimum return = (A + B)/2		
Chile	Risky funds (A & B) =	36 months	Monthly
	Min (50% of ARS; ARS −4%)		
	Conservative funds (C, D, & E) =		
	Min (50% of ARS; ARS −2%)		
Uruguay	Min (2% real rate, ARS −2%)	12 months	Monthly
Peru	Function of real ARS (prior to	60 months	Monthly
	multifondos' introduction)		

Source: Rudolph and others (2006).

ARS: average return of the system.

a. synthetic portfolio= its composition is prepared and updated by the pension superintendency.

ing and simplifying of quantitative investment limits, providing more flexibility in portfolio allocation.

Fee structure. The incentives for AFPs to maximize returns on affiliates' savings are limited by the weak link between AFP financial performance and revenues. In many countries, AFP revenues are largely independent of pension fund performance, with earnings coming mainly from contribution-based fees. While this fee structure ensures a sizable revenue stream to cover the relatively large operating expenses of young pension fund systems and provides incentives for AFPs to ensure active contributions by employers, it does little to motivate AFPs to optimize investment returns. In addition, there is some evidence that AFP affiliates do not actively follow comparative rates of return across AFPs (Berstein and Castro 2005) and that AFP market shares do not vary significantly with the rate of return (Rudolph and others 2006).

Performance-based commissions can create incentives for fund managers to maximize returns on affiliates' investments, but their efficacy has not been proven, and a complete shift to performance-based commissions could create undesirable adverse effects for affiliates. Commission schemes based partly on the performance of the fund have been considered as a mechanism for better aligning the incentives of pension fund managers and those of affiliates. So far, performance-related fees have played a minimal role even where they have been allowed (as in Mexico). There is a danger that performance-related commissions could penalize affiliates nearing retirement, because they have higher outstanding funds and would consequently pay higher commissions than young affiliates. As pension systems and securities markets mature, a more sophisticated fee structure comprising both contribution-based and performance-related fees might be economically sounder.

Finally, performance-based commissions require reasonably deep securities markets. The ability of AFPs to differentiate themselves based on their investment performance depends on the diversity of the investment instruments available to them, which remains quite constrained. In the current context, performance-based commissions would likely have a very limited impact on competition. It can be argued that the more active management is called on to be (the riskier and more complex), the higher the fees should be. However, the more that AFPs act as funds of funds or delegate active follow-up (for example, to securitization trustees), the lower the fees should be and attention should be paid to the incentives these choices create.

Minimum pension guarantee. Most Latin American countries with private pension funds provide some form of minimum pension guarantee. In Chile, the guarantee is about 25 percent of the average salary, while in Colombia and in Mexico, it is equal to the minimum wage. In Mexico, it is estimated that up to half of affiliates may exercise their minimum pension guarantee option, especially if a large proportion of affiliates contribute on the basis of the minimum wage and if private pension funds continue to invest conservatively in fixed-income securities instead of generating higher returns through equities investments (Sinha and Renteria 2005). Some argue that a minimum pension guarantee may pose a moral hazard problem by motivating risky investment strategies in individual accounts, given the existence of this downside protection (Smetters 2002). A minimum return guarantee partly mitigates the risk of unwise investments by AFPs when it includes an exogenous benchmark.

Interdependence of Defined Contribution Pension Systems and Domestic Capital Markets and the Momentum for Structured Finance

The value of assets under AFP management is substantial when compared with credit to GDP ratios in reforming Latin American countries, offering promise of a potential role in expanding investment in underserved productive sectors. But policymakers must refrain from directing these funds into unviable investments as part of an economic development strategy and from holding them hostage in domestic markets by unduly restricting foreign investments.

The regulatory authorities need to facilitate diversification of AFP portfolios by supporting the emergence of new private domestic securities. The regulatory authorities can support the development of the securities market by ensuring no unduly burdensome regulatory constraints on the issuance of new types of securities and no unjustifiably high transaction costs of issuance. Similarly, pension regulators should ensure that rules for AFPs clearly allow investment in new types of securities that meet minimum requirements for creditworthiness.

Many domestic capital markets remain small and have not kept up with AFP growth, creating risks of overvaluation of financials assets. Despite efforts to develop modern securities regulations and to foster stock markets and other securities-trading schemes, most markets remain shallow. Over the years, many successful local companies shifted their high-quality securities to international markets, further impeding the development of local capital markets. Many local markets thus have both insufficient depth and volume, with only a limited number of potential issuers that have the required credit quality to appeal to institutional investors such as AFPs. These may end up investing in financial assets with artificially high prices (low yields), with the added constraint that they have to compete for scarce investments with optimization-seeking foreign investors that can pursue globally diversified portfolios. In Colombia and Peru, high-quality corporate bonds can pay yields similar to or lower than government bonds—they are not adjusted for a liquidity premium—and local, limited liquidity stock markets have appreciated very fast (maybe too fast) over the last few years.

Recently, domestic capital markets have resumed growth as domestic issuance has substituted for foreign issuance. Domestic debt issuance has resumed in many countries, surpassing cross-border debt issuance for the first time in 2004. Declining domestic real interest rates and, more important, the rising volume of domestic savings have been credited for the turnaround. Domestic investors are often willing to invest in local instruments at lower yields than international investors are, due to a lower perception of sovereign risk and the absence of transfer and convertibility risks. However, the universe of highly rated issuers within each country and their issuance capacity remain limited, and thus high-quality, high-return investment opportunities have lagged behind the investment needs of AFPs.

Domestic structured finance transactions (especially through securitization) are starting to bring together institutional investors and new borrowers. In recent years, structured finance transactions have started to expand the universe of issuers and highly rated securities in several Latin American countries. Through widely accepted credit enhancement techniques (see appendix 1 for details), structured finance transactions have created securities with the high credit quality that pension funds require, while also providing direct access to capital markets to nontraditional sectors and issuers (figure 1.8). At the same time, structured finance mechanisms enable the development of multi-originator mechanisms that help produce securities with the critical mass to appeal to AFPs.

The volume of domestic structured finance transactions in Latin America increased significantly in 2004 and 2005. According to rating agencies,[16] structured finance issuance in Latin America in 2005 was on the order of US$14 billion (roughly equivalent to 8 percent of AFP assets), 96 percent of it issued locally. The volume of domestic issuance increased more than fivefold over 2004–05 (see figure 1.7). Brazil and Mexico jointly accounted for 72 percent of the volume of these domestic transactions in 2005 (figure 1.8). Going forward, Latin American markets are expected to maintain high growth in such transactions as new issuers enter the market and the industry develops in countries such as Argentina, Chile, Colombia, and Peru. Countries where the use of domestic securitizations has picked up have been aided by significant improvements in the local regulatory and legal frameworks (see annex 1.1).

The growth in structured finance transactions has been mutually beneficial. AFPs have been a main driver and investor in innovative structures, while structured finance transactions have enhanced pension fund diversification by bringing new asset classes to capital markets.[17] The flexibility of structured finance transactions enables institutional investors to participate in asset classes that would otherwise be unreachable. The issuance of structured debt instruments in Latin America has been concentrated largely in standardized assets such as residential mortgages and consumer loans originated by medium-size financial companies (figure 1.9). Similarly, a sizable number of transactions involve financing to large or medium-size enterprises through securitization of trade receivables and other financial assets.

The need for structured paper is driven not only by the need to diversify but also by the need to invest rapidly growing pools of domestically bound

Figure 1.7. Annual Volume of Securitization in Latin America

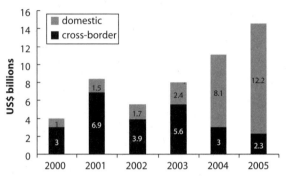

Source: Moody's Investors Service.

Note: Does not include project finance.

Figure 1.8. Country Shares of Domestic Securitization in 2005
(US$ billion)

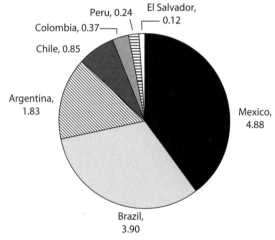

Source: Moody's Investors Service.

liquidity in high-quality papers. In countries where regulators have not been able to keep up with innovation and where AFPs can invest in private place-ments (for example, Peru), this has proved detrimental to price discovery, mark-to-market requirements, and secondary market development.

The primary requirement for successful securitization markets is the existence of a vast pool of cash flow–generating assets (a strong primary

Figure 1.9.   Composition of Domestic Securitization by Asset Type, 2005

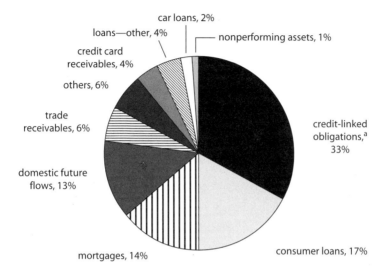

Source: Moody's Investors Service.

Note: These data do not include Chile's mortgage bonds since they are not securitizations.

a. Securitizations by Mexico's Institute for the Protection of Bank Savings.

market). First, securitizations entail significant transaction costs, including fees of investment banks acting as arrangers, underwriters, rating agencies, and trustees, among others.[18] Accordingly, the volume of the securitized portfolio must be great enough to ensure the economic viability of the transaction.[19,20] To date, transactions in Latin America have been above US$10 million on average, although smaller transactions have reached the market in Brazil (US$4.5 million), Peru (US$5 million), and Argentina (US$7.5 million). Securitizations also require fairly diversified portfolios to help mitigate the risk of concentration in a given loan, obligor, region, or industry. While portfolio concentration does not necessarily impede securitization, it translates into higher risk in the transactions and hence higher financing cost for originators. Securitizations can also change the overall credit risk profile of smaller originators because the highest-quality assets are frequently transferred to the market while the originator maintains those with highest risk. This problem is exacerbated in transactions where the originator maintains a subordinated participation.

Successful securitization markets have benefited from the development of appropriate legal frameworks and securities instruments. Authorities have played a major role in the development of securitization markets in Latin America. In Brazil and Mexico, the two most active markets, the large growth in issuances has been catalyzed in part by the development of new securities instruments that offer greater flexibility and cost efficiency to issuers as well as high security to investors (see annex 1.1). Other factors, such as a positive economic environment and market demand for new investment opportunities, have also been instrumental. In Chile, despite the size of the pension funds, securitization and credit-engineered bonds play a small role, except for mortgage-backed securities, creating the need for further investigation for each market.

The Way Forward

As countries seek to fine-tune their private pension fund regulations, they need to consider a number of important elements:

- Regulators have a vital role in promoting advanced risk management practices and good international practices in pension fund management.
- Pension fund regulation and capital market development activities should be tailored to specific country needs and realities, while benefiting from international and regional good practices.
- Regulators should avoid forcing pension savings to be invested exclusively in small domestic markets or directing them to particular assets or sectors for political reasons, especially when funds are growing too fast for their investment needs to be met by domestic assets alone.
- The authorities need to ease legal, regulatory, and tax obstacles to the development of soundly structured securities, as these are a promising class of assets that provides attractive risk-adjusted returns while meeting pension funds' requirement for creditworthy instruments to protect workers' savings.

Annex 1.1. The Enabling Role of Adequate Securitization Instruments

In Mexico, the introduction of "securities certificates" (*certificados bursátiles*, CBs) enabled the development of securitization markets. CBs are securities instruments created by Mexican authorities in 2001. For issuers, CBs provide highly flexible instruments whose flows and maturities can be easily adjusted to meet their financing needs. For investors, CBs provide a high level of security through the ability to incorporate covenants and accelerated amortization mechanisms. The creation of these instruments has been credited with significant growth in the bond market in Mexico over the past three years (figure A1.1).

CBs allow the creation of a special-purpose vehicle, which issues the bonds in the market.

Similarly, the strong growth in Brazilian domestic securitizations over the last couple of years was partly due to the promotion of a new instrument, the receivables investment fund (*fundo de investimento en dereitos creditorios*, FIDC). The FIDCs were made possible by a resolution of the monetary authority in 2001, with the rules governing their operation established by the Securities and Exchange Commission of Brazil. More than 91 FIDCs have reached the market since 2002, and by 2005, their combined value held by institutional investors had reached US$3.6 billion (figure A1.2). FIDCs have proved a flexible financing mechanism for Brazilian companies, providing an alternative to scarce bank credit at lower interest rates through securitization of credit rights.

Figure A1.1. Development of the Bond Market in Mexico through CBs

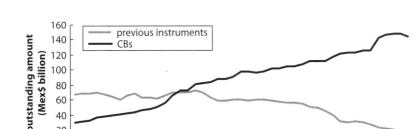

Source: Banco de México.

Note: Includes only debt issues of nonfinancial private companies.

Figure A1.2. Growth of the FIDC Market in Brazil, 2002–05

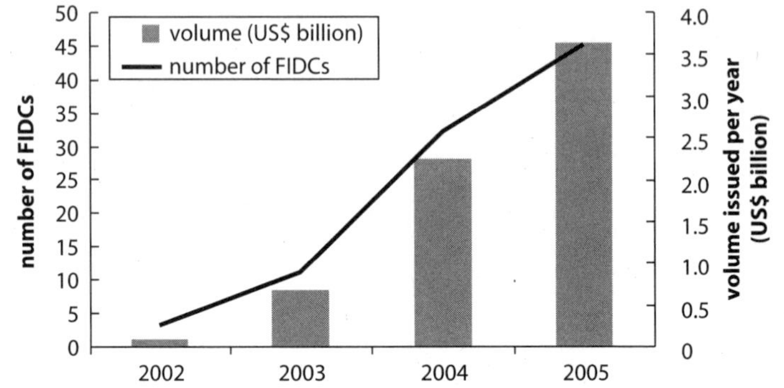

Source: Associação Nacional das Instituiçoes do Mercado Financiero.

Much of the success of the FIDCs is based on their adaptability to different economic sectors. They have been used in almost all sectors, as well as in some multisector transactions (figure A1.3). Similarly, the range of originators has expanded (including industrial companies, commercial firms, banks, and nonbank financial institutions), as FIDCs are suitable for many types of assets (trade receivables, letters of credit, car loans, purchases of durable goods on credit, personal loans, and other bank loans, among others). FIDCs can be tailored to the originators' financing needs and expected cash flows.

FIDCs function similarly to special-purpose vehicles, but work under the financial structure and administrative shell of a fund, which can be open-end or closed-end, with varying maturities (figure A1.4). The fund is managed by a creditworthy third party (usually a recognized financial institution), which is in charge of managing liquidity[21] to ensure prompt payment to senior investors. The originator of the transaction sells qualifying assets[22] to the FIDC at a discounted rate. This discount is in turn the source of the yield for the fund's investors.

For investors, FIDCs represent an investment opportunity with an appealing yield and a high level of creditworthiness. Investors' security is ensured through credit enhancement mechanisms such as subordination of shares[23] (usually maintained by originators to reduce moral hazard in the selection of assets sold to investors), covenants, and security margins. Because of the complexity of FIDCs, securities authorities in Brazil allow only institutional investors to purchase participation in an FIDC fund.

Figure A1.3. Number and Volume of FIDCs by Economic Sector of Originator, 2002–05

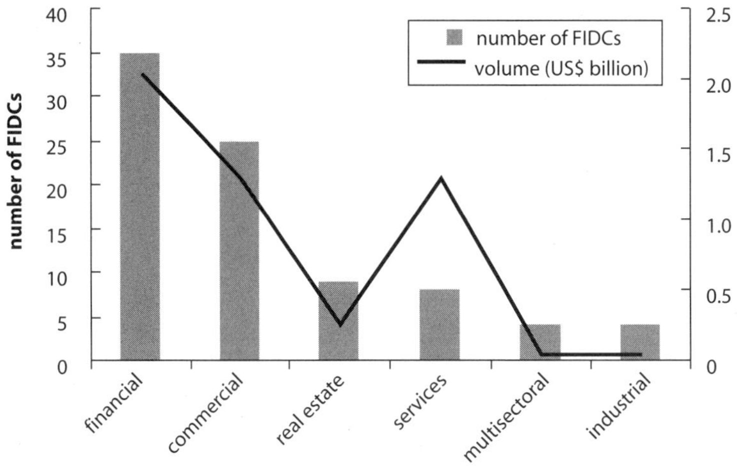

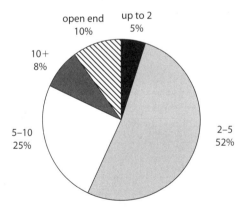

Source: Associãçao Nacional das Instituiçoes do Mercado Financiero.

Figure A1.4. Proportion of FIDCs by Maturity
(years)

open end 10% up to 2 5%
10+ 8%
5–10 25%
2–5 52%

Source: Associãçao Nacional das Instituiçoes do Mercado Financiero.

Note: This annex is based on information from FIDCs, "Estudos Especiais"; National Association of Financial Market Institutions (ANDIMA); *Gazeta Mercantil* (2006); and *Euromoney Yearbook* (2001).

Notes

1. Small debt issues can have limited appeal to AFPs, which may find it ineffi-cient to participate in these issues because of the operating costs of their investment decisions (including due diligence and internal analysis).

2. In Colombia workers can decide every five years whether to switch, whereas in Mexico workers must make a one-time switching decision at retirement.

3. Effective coverage refers to the proportion of the economically active popu-lation that contributes to pension funds.

4. Effective coverage is lower, all else being equal, in countries that allow exist-ing or new workers to switch to the unfunded public pillar.

5. Net investment returns should also be calculated (net of fees) to estimate actual performance, preferably after converting contribution-based fees into equivalent fees on assets. Otherwise, misleading negative net yields will be reached, especially for younger workers.

6. Evidence from Chile (Berstein and Chumacero 2005) shows that workers do not affect AFPs' investment allocation. The average worker in Latin America has neither the time nor the knowledge to have a meaningful impact on AFP investment strategies.

7. Upon retirement, the accumulated capital in the individual account has to be transformed into a stream of pension flows. If the retiree chooses to buy an annuity, the amount of the pension will be highly dependent on the long-term interest rate level at that time.

8. For instance, an entrepreneur has riskier human capital than a civil servant and therefore should invest less savings in equity.

9. Gómez, Jara, and Pardo (2005) for Colombia.

10. Publicly available portfolio data do not show the percentage in structured bonds. The last section of this chapter includes a more detailed account of structured finance issuance in Latin America.

11. Rating agencies' assessments are expressed in a rating scale that goes from AAA (the most creditworthy securities) to CCC (securities on the brink of default). "Investment-grade" ratings include AAA, AA, A, and BBB, which can have plus or minus modifiers to provide further granularity. Investment-grade ratings reflect a probability of timely and complete repayment that is at least "adequate."

12. Rating agencies usually have a local rating scale within each country that excludes the sovereign or convertibility risk and is therefore a valid bench-mark for domestic investors. These scales are usually differentiated from inter-national rating scales by a prefix (for example, "mx" in the case of Mexico). The highest rating is assigned to the debt issues of the government (for exam-

ple, mxAAA), and local issuers are ranked based on their creditworthiness relative to the sovereign.

13. For example, in Chile, most securities held by AFPs have a rating of at least A−, which is three levels above the minimum regulatory requirement.

14. Several countries, including Bolivia, El Salvador, and Mexico, have favored government bonds by disallowing or placing low limits on investments in corporate securities and foreign assets. In Argentina, authorities imposed higher holdings of government bonds on pension funds when the country faced the risk of imminent default.

15. As countries move toward implementing Basel 2, government debt may no longer be automatically weighted at zero risk. For example, under the Basel 2 standardized approach, the weight will depend on the credit rating given to the government.

16. Rating agencies have been the main source of information on structured finance activities in the region; official information from regulatory bodies is hard to obtain.

17. Data on ownership of structured notes by class of investors are not available. This conclusion is based on rating agency reports and discussions with industry.

18. Another cost of securitized or otherwise engineered bonds is the need to pay for a specific annual, updated risk rating per issue (as opposed to rating update of the issuing firm that is applicable to all its ordinary securities).

19. Zervos (2004) estimates the one-off transaction costs (excluding interest) of small ordinary debt issues at between 1.99 percent and 4.75 percent of the amount issued in different countries in Latin America. This cost would be amortized over the life of the bonds. Given the complexity of the securitizations, it can be expected that transaction costs could be higher, but this is hard to quantify and likely depends on the complexity of the transaction.

20. The transaction costs in securitizations usually include the fees of the investment bank structuring the transaction; internal cost to the originator, including the segregation, accounting, and monitoring of assets to securitize; the fees of rating agencies (two ratings are needed in some countries); the fees to the manager of the special-purpose vehicle; potential higher cost of regulatory approvals; opportunity cost (if pledges) or direct cost (if purchased guarantee) of credit enhancements; opportunity cost of building liquidity reserve; and opportunity cost of idle asset flows built up to meet bond servicing.

21. The fund manager can incorporate a combination of receivables (representing at least 50 percent of the fund's total assets) and debt securities.

22. Assets sold to the FIDC must meet a clearly defined set of criteria to ensure that the credit quality of the FIDC portfolio remains stable throughout its operations.

23. Subordination refers to a prioritized collection of securities issued. The risk of the reference portfolio is sliced into two or more tranches, with the most junior tranche (commonly known as the first loss position) bearing any initial loses. If tranches are subordinated, any losses in excess of the lower tranche are absorbed by the subsequent tranche, and so on, leaving the most senior tranches with only a remote probability of being affected by defaults in the reference portfolio. The cash flows generated by the underlying assets are assigned to investors according to their seniority. So, senior tranches carry a high rating, provided that junior tranches are issued in sufficient proportions.

References

Benzoni, Luca, Pierre Collin-Dufresne, and Robert S. Goldstein. 2004. "Portfolio Choice over the Life Cycle in the Presence of 'Trickle Down' Labor Income." NBER Working Paper W11247, National Bureau of Economic Research, Cambridge, MA.

Berstein, Solange, and Rubén Castro. 2005. "Costos y rentabilidad de los fondos de pensiones: ¿Qué Informar a los Aliados?" Documento de trabajo 1, Superintendencia de AFP, Santiago.

Berstein, Solange, and Rómulo Chumacero. 2005. "Cuantificación de los costos de los límites de inversión para los fondos de pensiones chilenos." Documento de trabajo 3, Superintendencia de AFP, Santiago.

Bodie, Zvi. 2005a. "Observations on Personal Retirement Accounts." In *Proceedings*, Federal Reserve Bank of Chicago, 108–16.

———. 2005b. "Pension Insurance." DNB Working Papers 066, Netherlands Central Bank, Research Department, Amsterdam.

International Association of Latin American Pension Funds Supervisors (AIOS). 2004. Statistical Bulleting No. 12. http://www.aiosfp.org/estadisticas/boletines_estadisticos/boletin12.pdf, accessed in March 2007.

International Association of Latin American Pension Funds Supervisors (AIOS). June 2005. Statistical Bulleting No. 13. http://www.aiosfp.org/estadisticas/boletines_estadisticos/boletin13.pdf, accessed in March 2007.

International Association of Latin American Pension Funds Supervisors (AIOS). December 2005. Statistical Bulleting No. 14. http://www.aiosfp.org/estadisticas/boletines_estadisticos/boletin14.pdf, accessed in March 2007.

Gómez, Carolina, Diego Jara, and Andres Pardo. 2005. "Análisis de eficiencia de los portafolios pensiónales obligatorios en Colombia." Ensayos sobre Política Económica, Banco de la República de Colombia, Bogotá.

Iglesias, Augusto. 2004. "La Regulación de las inversiones de los fondos de pensiones en América Latina." In *Inversión de los Fondos de Pensiones*, 27–47. FIAP.

Jara, Diego. 2006. "Modelo de la regulación de las AFP en Colombia y su impacto en el portafolio de los fondos de pensiones." Banco de la República de Colombia, Bogotá.

Rudolph, Heinz, Hela Cheikhrouhou, Roberto Rocha, and Craig Thorburn. 2006. "Financial Sector Dimensions of the Colombian Pension System." World Bank, Washington, DC.

Shiller, Robert J. 2005. "The Life-Cycle Personal Accounts Proposal for Social Security: An Evaluation."

Sinha, Tapen, and Alejandro Renteria. 2005. "The Cost of Minimum Pension Guarantee." http://ssrn.com/abstract=839213 SSRN, accessed March 2007.

Smetters, Kent. 2002. "Controlling the Cost of Minimum Benefit Guarantees in Public Pensions Conversions." NBER Working Paper 8732, National Bureau of Economic Research, Cambridge, MA.

Viceira, Luis. 2001. "Optimal Portfolio Choice for Long-Horizon Returns with Non-Tradable Labor Income." *Journal of Finance* 56: 433–70.

Walker, Eduardo.2006. "Strategic Currency Hedging and Global Portfolio Investments: An Upside Down View." FIAP.

Zervos, Sara. 2004. "The Transaction Costs of Primary Market Issuance: The Case of Brazil, Chile , and Mexico." Policy Research Working Paper 3424, World Bank, Washington, DC.

CHAPTER 2

Structured Finance for Housing

After many years of trying and despite significant barriers, a few Latin American countries have developed mortgage-related securities markets. Success requires a strong legal and regulatory framework, a liberalized financial sector, and an active primary mortgage market. This chapter presents reasons to develop mortgage securities, a few of the more recent successful cases, and the critical success factors in developing mortgage securities markets (Chiquier, Hassler, and Lea 2004).

The traditional model of housing finance has failed in Latin America, sometimes spectacularly. Inflation and defects in the indexation formula bankrupted Colombia's savings and loan system. Brazil's heavily regulated system of submarket-rate lenders has not been able to finance housing for the majority of the population. State-owned housing banks making direct loans have been notorious for submarket pricing and weak collections, leading to large losses in Argentina, Uruguay, Ecuador, Colombia, and Peru. State-owned providential funds, which combine pension savings and housing loans, have also had a long and checkered history of submarket pricing, poor collections, and negative real pension payouts, as in Brazil and Mexico.

A market-based system of mortgage funding coupled with well-targeted and transparent subsidies can develop housing finance for a wide range of the population. The best example in Latin America is Chile, and Mexico and Colombia have made substantial progress. Incomes have risen in much of Latin America with improved economic growth and macroeconomic stability. Countries that provide a constructive policy framework for private sector mortgage lending can reach a much broader part of the population than has ever been possible with public funds.

The Latin American countries that have had success in developing mortgage securities have done so with securitization—with one important exception. That exception, Chile, boasts a successful history of mortgage bonds issuance, but mortgage securitization has grown more recently. Mexico and Colombia have each produced repeat issues of mortgage-backed security. Argentina is rebounding from the crisis that accompanied the demise of the currency peg and the subsequent devaluation in 2002. Peruvian banks have securitized a number of asset classes, including mortgages.

Housing and Housing Finance

Real estate markets in developing countries are not adequately meeting the rising need for shelter and urban infrastructure. By 2008, the world is projected to become more than half urban. The population of cities in developing countries is expected to increase by more than a billion in the next 15 years (Buckley and Kalarickal 2005). In Latin America, the supply of serviced urban land and low-cost housing has not kept up with urbanization, restricting the supply of shelter for the poor. The result: large qualitative and quantitative housing deficits. In Mexico, 4.2 million households live in inadequate conditions; in Peru, 1.2 million households; and in Brazil, 50 million individuals (Comisión Nacional de Fomento de Vivienda México, Titularizadora Colombiana 2005). Frustrated urban poor have settled illegally on public and private land, creating substandard shantytowns surrounding most cities. These informal settlements, where the inhabitants lack legal title to their homes, also generally lack connections to water, sanitation, and electricity.

Cities are built the way they are financed (Renaud 1987). The growth of shantytowns results from low incomes, inefficient primary real estate markets, and inadequate real estate financing. In the best of circumstances, a completed house may cost a moderate- or low-income borrower two to five times his or her annual income. In developed countries, low-income households either rent housing—sometimes with the benefit of subsidies to landlords—or buy housing using mortgage finance, again sometimes with the benefit of subsidies. In Latin America, real estate markets generally do not provide rental housing on a large scale for the poor. A limited number of households benefit from purchase subsidy programs in several countries. But for the vast majority, restrictions on land markets limit the supply of land near cities.

Since 60 percent or more of the population of Latin America have no contact with banks or other lenders, they are not able to get a mortgage or save for a down payment. Most urban slum dwellers lack legal title, and so cannot mortgage their property, even if they feel comfortable entering a bank. As a result, the urban poor build their houses progressively, starting with a parcel of land and a basic shelter, and adding or improving components as they are able. Without access to financial services, the poor save using building materials. Where governments enable responsive real estate markets and financial systems, the private sector does more in providing housing solutions to the urban poor.

Mortgage finance in many Latin American countries reaches only households in the top fifth of the population, even though many more households could afford a mortgage, given longer maturities and relatively low interest rates. Few Latin Americans use formal sector financial institutions. In Mexico in 2004, 75 percent of Mexican households lacked a deposit account (Caskey, Duran, and Solo 2006). In Colombia, 61 percent of the adult population lacks access to any financial services (Solo and Manroth 2006). Widespread informality of employment, distrust of institutions, and minimum bank account size have kept most low- and moderate-income individuals away from banks. But programs in some countries have shown that moderate- and low-income households can afford mortgages. In Mexico, government funding, subsidies, and mortgage default insurance have extended market lending to the 50th percentile with 20-year loans. Banks historically lent only to those in the top fifth, typically for 15 years or less. Improved financing techniques, such as mortgage securities, make mortgage finance more accessible for moderate-income households by reducing risk for lenders.

In most Latin American countries, systemwide mortgage portfolios range from only 2 to 6 percent of GDP. In developed countries, 20- and 30-year fixed- and floating-rate mortgages enable a broad range of the population to consume housing, and they provide a safe and liquid asset for banks. In Western Europe and North America, systemwide mortgage portfolios average about 40 percent of GDP, reaching as high as 70–90 percent. In developing countries that have had some success developing mortgage markets, such as Mexico and Chile, mortgages total 11 percent of GDP.

Mortgage Securities Channel Long-Term Funds from Institutional Investors and Improve Allocation of Risk within the Financial System
Mortgage securities increase the flow of funds to the housing sector and better allocate the risks in housing finance. In economies with pools of contractual savings funds, mortgage securities tap these as funds for housing (box 2.1). Institutional investors (pension and insurance funds) with long-term liabilities are potentially important sources of funds for housing because they can manage the liquidity risk of housing loans more effectively than can short-funded depository institutions.

In Chile, mortgage bonds have been important as an investment instrument for insurers and pension funds—and as a means to channel long-term housing finance. Mortgages of up to 25-year maturity have been available in Chile since the 1970s, funded by *letras de crédito hipotecario,*

Box 2.1

Defining Mortgage Bonds and Mortgage-Backed Securities

In this chapter, "mortgage securities" refers both to on-balance-sheet mortgage bonds (also known as covered bonds, *cedulas hipotecarias,* or *letras hipotecarias*) and to off-balance-sheet mortgage securitizations (commonly referred to as mortgage-backed securities). Each instrument provides long-term financing based on the cash flow of a portfolio of mortgages. Each structure has its advantages, depending on circumstances. Ideally, the legal and regulatory framework should provide a choice between the two based on the financial features of each instrument, without artificial advantages through taxes or regulatory restrictions.

Mortgage bond. A mortgage bond is a senior general obligation issue of the bank backed by a specified pool of residential mortgages on its balance sheet. Mortgage bonds are effective where lenders have the market standing to issue bonds. Should the issuing bank fail, the collateral pool for the mortgage bond is separated from the assets of the bank and is available only to satisfy the claims of the mortgage bondholders. This "ring fencing" of collateral is essential to the pricing and quality of the issue, as is the overall financial strength of the issuing bank.

Where banks have the market standing to issue bonds, the mortgage bond structure and ring fencing of collateral can increase the bond rating by one or more notches, reducing the cost of funding. For ring fencing of collateral to be effective, most countries require a special law for its establishment. Mortgage

Box 2.1 (*continued*)

bonds may be pass-through securities, as in Chile and Denmark, where all cash flows are passed to investors, whether they are scheduled payments, prepayments, or defaults. More commonly, they are pay-through, where the bonds have a simplified payment structure similar to that of a standard corporate bond, such as semiannual interest payments and principal at maturity.

In general, mortgage lenders keep mortgages on their balance sheets as safe, long-term investments if they can fund them safely. Banks in Latin America would fund with mortgage bonds, but few countries have created an adequate legal framework. Where legal backing for mortgage bonds exists, as in Colombia and Chile, it is often accompanied by restrictions (such as the pass-through requirement) that makes the structure less attractive than securitization.

Mortgage-backed security. Issuers of mortgage-backed securities sell the pool of mortgage loans to a trust or other specially created legal entity (special-purpose vehicle). The special-purpose vehicle then issues bonds. The collateral pool must be completely removed from the balance sheet of the issuer in an arm's length transaction that reflects market pricing of the assets. There can be no recourse to the seller in the case of default of mortgages in the collateral pool, nor may the seller view the collateral pool as a resource in case of need. If the seller goes bankrupt, the seller's creditors have no access to assets of the special-purpose vehicle. Since the pool of a mortgage-backed security stands alone, financially weak institutions can securitize assets and raise cash, unlike mortgage bonds.

Mortgage-backed securities may be pass-through securities, where all cash flows are passed to investors, whether they are scheduled payments, prepayments, or defaults, or they may be pay-through, where separate bonds convey distinct rights to the cash flows of the collateral pool. In a pay-through mortgage-backed security, the issuer typically creates senior bonds and subordinate bonds. In the simplest pay-through structures, senior bonds receive scheduled interest and principal, as well as principal prepayments. Subordinate bonds receive cash flows only after the scheduled payments and prepayments are allocated to the senior bonds. The subordinate bonds suffer first from defaults, and their receipt of interest payments is reduced by any prepayments. Mortgage-backed securities are popular partly because the structuring allows cash flows to be allocated in an infinite number of ways, allowing the issuer to tailor the bonds to the precise needs of institutional investors.

which are covered bonds typically indexed to inflation—responding to annuity providers' need to preserve the purchasing power of pensioners—but with the legal possibility of denomination in pesos. Chile supported the *letras* system by creating a liquidity facility that could buy *letras*. In 1980, when Chile created a fully funded pension system with individual retirement accounts, it also permitted insurance companies to sell annuities backed by *letras* as investments for the retirement accounts in the payout phase of the privatized pension system.

As market conditions changed, particularly the taxation and regulatory framework, Chile moved away from mortgage bonds and toward securitization. The government eliminated stamp taxes on refinancing, making it more attractive for individuals to take advantage of steep declines in interest rates between 2000 and 2004 (SBIF 2006). Prepayment rates rose dramatically, reaching an annualized 39.8 percent for prime mortgages in November 2004 (Fitch Ratings 2005). Likewise, stamp taxes on securitization were eliminated, changing the cost-benefit calculus for mortgage bonds and securitization. The pass-through feature of *letras* proved difficult for institutional investors to manage as prepayments rose. Securitization is more flexible for banks, as they have begun to offer a wider range of loan products. There are also more legal restrictions on mortgages funded with *letras* than on other kinds. At the end of 2005, 39 percent of mortgages were financed with *letras*, down from 67 percent in 2003 and 70 percent in 2001. Institutional investors are major buyers of mortgage-backed securities, just as they were of *letras*.

Motivations for Issuing Mortgage Securities

Mortgage-Backed Securities Provided Liquidity to Colombian Lenders in the Wake of the 1998 Crisis

Financial crises spurred reforms in several countries. As one of the measures to recover from its 1998 financial crisis, Colombia passed legislation that facilitated mortgage securitization and the creation of a standalone company that could buy portfolios from banks and issue securities with the portfolios as collateral.[1] Securitization was seen as a means to supply liquidity and risk diversification for mortgage lenders, and it was an important tool for restructuring the mortgage lending industry in the wake of the crisis. But it did not lead to growth in the primary market, which stalled in the wake of the crisis. So, securitization follows the development of primary markets, but it cannot be expected to stimulate one in the absence of demand for (or supply of) mortgages.

The securitization conduit Titularizadora Colombiana, since its creation in 2002, has securitized about 30 percent of outstanding mortgages. About half the resulting bonds have been sold to insurance companies, finance companies, and—to a lesser extent—pension funds (Titularizadora Colombiana 2005). This allocates credit and interest rate risk away from the originating banks and provides institutional investors with longer-duration investments that better match long-term liabilities (for insurance companies).[2] Risks remain, including the slow recovery of lending, linked to the persistence of ceilings on mortgage interest rates set by the Constitutional Court.

Access to alternative sources of funds through the capital markets may allow lenders to continue to provide housing finance even as deposits are withdrawn from the system. Lenders relying on deposits may be subject to periodic outflows due to economic downturns or widening differentials between deposit and alternative investment rates (for example, if deposit rates are regulated).

Securitization Can Provide the Means for Nonbank Financial Institutions to Compete against Banks

Mortgage securities can increase competition in primary markets. Capital market funding frees lenders from having to develop expensive retail funding sources (branch networks) to mobilize funds. Securitization can allow small, thinly capitalized lenders that specialize in mortgage origination and servicing to enter the market. These lenders can increase competition in the market for originations, introducing lower margins and product innovations. In Australia, the entry of wholesale-funded specialist lenders led to a reduction of 200 basis points in mortgage spreads from 1994 to 1996.

In Mexico, Sociedad Hipotecaria Federal originally catalyzed the primary market by fostering mortgage nonbank finance companies that are not permitted to take deposits. Banks withdrew entirely from mortgage lending in the wake of the financial crisis of 1995, but nonbank finance companies (*sociedades financieras de objeto limitado*, or SOFOLs) continued to lend to moderate-income households, funded by Sociedad Hipotecaria Federal. While some SOFOLs have grown large enough to issue securities on their own, the industry remains fragile in the face of competition from deposit-funded banks. With Sociedad Hipotecaria Federal's credit line ending in 2009, the future of smaller SOFOLs is unclear.

Links to Broader Fixed-Income Markets—Repurchase Agreements and Mortgage-Related Securities

Liquidity management tools can increase the appetite of investors for fixed-income securities. Consider repurchase agreements ("repos"), collateralized loans that use debt securities for collateral.[3] Repurchase agreements foster a more active bond market (through continuous pricing and a more developed secondary market) and make the capital market a less onerous source of financing (through lower liquidity premiums than bank loans, because of the possibility for the investor to repurchase securities to obtain financing).

Mortgage-backed securities can serve as repurchase agreement collateral where production of homogeneously defined securities is consistent. The European Central Bank System allows banks to use mortgage bonds as collateral for repurchase transactions for monetary policy purposes within the euro zone. In Colombia, mortgage-backed securities are eligible as collateral for repurchase agreements with an interest rate hedging facility run by the central bank.

Risks of Mortgage Securities

The earnings of mortgage securities are based on the cash flows of the underlying pools of mortgages. As a result, the investor's yield on a mortgage security may be affected by default risk, market risk, and operational risk.

Default Risk

Even though mortgage loans are secured by the pledged property, the enforcement of the pledge is expensive and will lead to losses in just about any environment. Mortgage lenders in most countries, developed or emerging, will go to great lengths to avoid enforcing a mortgage lien in court. It is almost always cheaper for the lender to come to terms with the borrower—for instance, by renegotiating the maturity or interest rate of the loan, or by negotiating a sale of the property and prepaying the loan— than go to the expense of a court case, eviction, and eventual sale of the property.

Investors in mortgage securities may or may not be protected against default risk. Some mortgage bonds commit the issuer to replace defaulted mortgages in the collateral pool with performing loans (securitization with recourse to the originator). Most pay-through mortgage-backed securities structures protect the senior bondholders against default risk by prioritizing the principal and interest payments for the senior bonds. But if default rates rise high enough, as in a financial crisis, even senior bond-holders may suffer from default risk.

Market Risk

The cash flows of a mortgage security may vary as a result of the level of interest rates and the state of the economy. When interest rates fall or economic conditions are good, borrowers may prepay their loans in whole or in part. In much of Latin America, homeowners prefer to pay off mortgages as quickly as possible to reduce their indebtedness, so they make regular partial prepayments. When economic circumstances are difficult or interest rates are rising, mortgage borrowers may reduce prepayments and return to the original scheduled payments. As the duration of the mortgage security varies, so does the expected yield to the investor.

When mortgage pools prepay, mortgage security investors are deprived of the interest income they would have earned on the outstanding principal over the contractual maturity. As mentioned previously, Chilean *letras* recently prepaid at 50 percent annual rates. Recent issues of mortgage-backed securities in Colombia have experienced 8 percent annual prepayment rates on the underlying collateral pool. After allocations to separate classes of senior and subordinate bonds, some of the nominally five-year bonds pay off in as little as a year. While the credit risk is low (the investor receives the entire invested principal), the market risk is high (the investor must replace four years of interest income, but mortgages are typically prepaid more when the alternative investment yields are lower).[4]

Currency risk arises through exposure to foreign currency, as when debt is denominated in dollars while individuals earn local currency. With rapid depreciation or devaluation, such exposure increases credit risk. In Argentina, the collapse of the currency peg in 2001 was accompanied by the conversion of debt at the parity exchange rate, which benefited individuals who happened to keep dollar deposits abroad, generally the middle and upper classes. The debt conversion at the parity rate hurt lenders, leading to the default of mortgage-backed securities collateralized by local currency loans but issued in dollars.

Mortgages may be indexed to inflation, creating additional default risks in times of extremely high inflation, but also creating potential for one of the asset classes sought by annuity providers and private pension fund managers. Inflation-indexed mortgages provide the basis for securities that are ideal for long-term institutional investors. Chile, Colombia, and Mexico are prominent users of inflation indexation. Chile's system succeeded in part because almost the entire financial system was indexed, and in part because inflation has been reduced dramatically over the past 20 years. Colombia's indexing system lasted from the early 1970s until 1998, when interest rates spiked during the financial system crisis and the mortgage index, linked in part to short-term rates, also spiked, driving up monthly payments. Defaults rose to 33 percent of outstanding loans. Mexico's indexing system was restructured in the wake of the 1995 peso crisis. In Mexico, though indexed mortgages remain the primary instrument for moderate-income borrowers, fixed-rate peso mortgages are now gaining in popularity because inflation has been reduced to less than 5 percent.

Operational Risk

Unlike consumer or commercial lending, mortgages remain outstanding for 10 or 20 years, with important legal documentation requirements. Some of the largest losses in mortgage credit crises have resulted from inadequate documentation of the mortgage lien by lenders.[5] The mortgage servicer and the bond administrator have to maintain tight controls over their business and financial processes for thousands of loans over hundreds of months. Mortgage-backed securities investors lose earnings if servicers fail to collect on the loans that back the issue, or if they have persistent errors or inefficiencies in processing the cash flows. Rating agencies monitor the performance of mortgage-backed securities transactions over their life and will reduce the rating on a bond that suffers from inefficient servicing. Sociedad Hipotecaria Federal has promulgated agency ratings of the servicing capabilities of Mexican SOFOLs, leading to greater expertise and transparency. High-quality servicing capacity is an essential link in the value chain for mortgage securitization.

Steps to Make Securitization Feasible

From the Issuer's Standpoint

For securitization to be sustainable, a market need for capital market funding must be clear. It is almost always the case that capital market (wholesale) funding is more expensive than retail (typically deposit) funding on a debt-only, nonrisk-adjusted basis. Even so, capital market funding may be attractive for several reasons:

- *Capital-constrained lenders.* When lenders are capital constrained, the all-in costs of wholesale funding may be less than those of retail funding, taking into account the high expense of equity capital. This was so for Colombian mortgage lenders immediately after the 1998 financial crisis. To finance their diversification into new business lines and improve their capital positions, it was worthwhile for them to securitize some of their mortgages to benefit from capital relief, even though they enjoyed relatively inexpensive deposit funding.[6] In another case, smaller Peruvian banks look to Fondo MiVivienda to use its credit enhancements to facilitate pools large enough to warrant the cost of securitization.

- *Liquidity and asset-liability management needs.* Lenders may be short of liquidity or may wish to offer products whose characteristics are difficult to manage through traditional retail means, such as medium- or long-term fixed-rate mortgages. Chilean lenders turned to *letras* in the 1980s and 1990s—and more recently to mortgage-backed securities— to safely fund long-term mortgage lending. Colombian mortgage lenders, in the wake of the crisis, improved their liquidity by securitizing the bulk of the nonperforming mortgages remaining on their balance sheet. A motivation to securitize was the mismatch between short-term nominal rate deposits and 20-year inflation-adjusted mortgages. In Peru, larger banks are overliquid, so they are content to retain mortgages on the balance sheet. Smaller Peruvian banks that would benefit from securitization lack the scale to assemble individual pools large enough to justify the costs.[7]

- *Improving risk management and transparency.* As regulators require banks to manage and mitigate market and credit risk, mortgage securitization becomes more important to bank managers. Arm's length sales transactions, either through mortgage bonds or securitization, encourage more accuracy and transparency in costing and managing the origination, servicing, and holding of mortgages. In Colombia, the banking authority imposed higher capital requirements for banks that hold interest rate exposure on their books in the form of asset-liability mismatches. Banks can reduce mismatches by securitizing mortgages, by issuing mortgage bonds, or simply by issuing long-term inflation-indexed corporate bonds. Colombia's Banco Davivienda benefits from its strong market presence to do all three. In combination with its deposit base, it now has a mix of funding strategies to achieve a well-balanced portfolio and optimize its risk-adjusted capital allocation. Banks without Davivienda's market presence or without a strong credit rating can raise funding by selling portfolios to the mortgage securitization conduit.

For mortgage securitization to succeed, a class of investors must have an appetite and capacity for securities backed by mortgages. Mexican mortgage-backed securities have been purchased by insurance companies in Mexico, private pension plans, and by Chilean insurance companies. Peruvian pension funds (as well as life insurers providing annuities) would be happy to buy Peruvian mortgage-backed securities. In Colombia, roughly half the demand comes from other lenders and half from insurance companies, finance companies, and pension funds.[8] Some countries, may have a geographic mismatch—for example, some lenders may be asset rich and others liability rich (historically the case in the large U.S. market). The development of a secondary mortgage market can facilitate the movement of funds between regions. The demand most likely will come from institutional investors, such as insurance companies or pension funds that have long-term liabilities.

Mortgage securities must offer attractive risk-adjusted returns. In most cases, institutional investors will look to mortgage securities as an alternative to government bonds. In Latin American capital markets, government bonds are generally the predominant fixed-income security, providing a benchmark yield because they represent a relatively default-risk-free, relatively liquid investment alternative.[9] Mortgage security investors will seek a premium over government bond yields to reflect credit risk, liquidity risk, prepayment risk, and transaction costs of purchasing and managing the assets. The premium required by investors may be reduced if credit enhancement is credible (either by third parties or through structuring) and if markets are liquid (if there are market makers, a function often served by broker-dealers, committed to trade at posted prices with acceptable bid-offer spreads). Mortgage securities can also be an alternative to high-quality corporate bonds.

Investors must have the financial capacity to buy mortgage-related securities. When government debt absorbs a large part of private sector capital, the capacity of institutional investors to purchase mortgage securities may be limited or nonexistent (the government may crowd out other issuers). Capacity may also be related to the liability mix of investors, who may prefer short-duration assets in volatile environments to minimize the price risk in their portfolios, again highlighting the importance of a sound macroeconomic environment. In recent years, as inflation subsided in most Latin American countries, insurers and pension funds expressed greater interest in long-term paper (expecting capital gains from further yield drops). Colombian mortgage-backed securities issues were all oversubscribed, some by as much as two or three times. In Mexico, the creation of private pension funds and the downward trend in local rates generated opportunistic demand for long-term paper. The introduction of private pension accounts in Chile spurred demand for mortgage-related securities in the absence of other investment instruments. As capital markets developed, Chilean pension funds diversified into other asset classes, but *letras* remain an important institutional investment and the dominant form of mortgage funding. In markets that lack private pension systems (such as Guatemala) or large insurance industries, banks are the main buyers of mortgage bonds.[10]

Investors must be permitted to invest in mortgage-based securities. Investors must have the legislative and regulatory authority to invest in such assets. And the regulatory treatment—for capital adequacy, liquidity and asset allocation, and eligibility for technical reserves—must be well defined and accurately reflect risk. As explained in chapter 1, the regulatory framework, such as a minimum performance benchmark, should not force investors managing long-term funds to prefer shorter-term and liquid securities. Chilean, Mexican, and Colombian pension fund and insurance regulators each permit investments in long-term mortgage-related securities. Colombian capital adequacy rules reflect the credit risk rating and subordination of securitization bonds. In Mexico, private pension funds have been quick to invest in mortgage-backed securities. But in Colombia, the most important institutional demand has not come from pension funds, because they do not benefit from the tax exemption of interest earned on mortgage-backed securities.

Necessary Legal and Regulatory Conditions
Even if there are willing issuers and investors, infrastructure requirements underlie the development of mortgage capital markets. Most important are the legal prerequisites.

Ability to enforce liens. Because investors eventually bear the credit risk of mortgages underlying a security, the enforceability of the mortgage pledge is a major determinant of the security's attractiveness. It is no accident that the countries with the most developed housing finance systems, defined by the availability of mortgage credit and its cost, are those with legal systems that strongly enforce property rights. Foreclosure, including efforts to renegotiate or sell the property and repeated notices to the borrower, may take as little as three months in Denmark or the United States. While foreclosure is almost always a money-losing proposition, lenders need to be able to enforce contracts. During financial crises, such as those in Argentina, Colombia, and Mexico, high levels of defaults extended over years. In Colombia and Mexico, frequent defaults were connected with political movements creating cultures of nonpayment. In each case, it took some time to reestablish relationships between lenders and moderate- and low-income individuals.

The challenge is balancing the protection of consumer and creditor rights. Often in Latin America, the tendency has been to err on the side of consumer protection, with foreclosure periods stretching beyond five years, harming consumer access to finance. By contrast, in the United States, foreclosure time ranges from as little as three months to a year, with six to nine months the norm. Research in the United States and Europe shows that where foreclosure times are shorter, larger mortgage loans are made at lower interest rates (Jappelli, Pagano, and Bianco 2002; Pence 2003). In recent years, Mexico and Colombia passed packages of laws to reduce the average time to foreclosure from five years to about two. These packages reduced documentary requirements to establish the existence of a lien and simplified the requirements for notifying borrowers that they are in default. Mexico permits lenders to circumvent local courts and take foreclosure cases to federal commercial courts, which have lower caseloads. Similar commercial courts are being tested in Peru.

Facilities for lien registration and the ability to transfer (assign) security interests. Since mortgage securities are backed by mortgage loans, recording the lender's interest in the collateral and the transfer of that interest to the security holder must be accurate, timely, and moderate in cost. For securitization, the legal system must recognize and record the transfer of the lender's beneficial interest to the investor at a modest cost. For mortgage bonds, the ability to transfer beneficial interest is important in the event of issuer bankruptcy. Any requirement to notify the borrower that the beneficial interest has been transferred should be relatively easy and inexpensive for the transferor—say, by advertising in a broadly read newspaper.

Extensive efforts to modernize property and lien registration in several Latin American countries have achieved varying success. Securitization in large, federal countries (Mexico) has not developed as quickly as desired, in part because local governments have not managed property and lien registrations consistently. Even after all its reforms, the Peruvian title registry system will need further investment to be able to quickly register lien transfers in large quantities.

Adequate taxation, accounting, and legal framework for securitization and secured bond issuance. The accounting and tax treatment of mortgage securities for issuers and investors must be clear and complete and should reflect international best practices. The International Financial Reporting Standards provide guidance to establish the "true sale" status of securitizations. Basel 2 standards for asset securitization also provide guidance for recognizing transactions. And in countries where rating agencies are active, Basel 2 provides a framework for holding capital against bank investments in securitization tranches. Regulators should establish standards for adequate disclosure of information on the collateral and the issuer in the offering documents. Subsequent monitoring reports are necessary to assess risk at the time of security purchase and—over time—to assess collateral performance.

Protection of investors against bankruptcy of originator or servicer. The credibility of legal provisions that ensure bondholders of the bankruptcy remoteness of collateral is critical to the success of either mortgage bonds or mortgage-backed securities.[11] For mortgage bonds, in case of issuer bankruptcy, the collateral backing the bonds must be separated (ring fenced) from other assets made available to general creditors. In Chile, this was achieved through specific legislation and subsequent regulation by the central bank.[12]

For securitization a special-purpose vehicle or other construct that isolates the collateral pool from the issuer or servicer is essential to obtain off-balance-sheet accounting and better capital treatment for the issuer. Special-purpose vehicles are often absent in developing-country law, so to simplify and promote securitization, many jurisdictions legislate them into existence. For instance, the Colombian Congress created a special-purpose vehicle (a *universalidad*), which exists as a legal person with limited capacities and is bankruptcy remote from its creator and administrator.

Primary market practices. Secondary markets cannot develop without sound primary market practices. A mortgage bond or mortgage-backed security is nothing more than the rights to the cash flows from a pool of individual loans. If the loan pool is of poor quality, so will be the mortgage-related security.

Standardization of lending documents and underwriting practices. The more standardized the loan products, legal documents, and underwriting practices, the lower the transaction costs of due diligence and credit enhancements in securitization. This constraint is less stringent for mortgage bonds, which shift the emphasis of standardization from the loans to the securities. But it is essential that legal frameworks for mortgage bonds define clear, high-quality lending requirements.

Standardizing collateral and bond structures contributes to comparability, making it easier to derive mark-to-market reference pricing and thus reducing yield premiums on mortgage securities. Since standardization requires lenders to change their business processes and automated systems, it is expensive and must be worth the investment. Bankers are more likely to standardize processes because of economic incentives than regulatory directives. In the United States, the mortgage lending standards that are now universally accepted were originally promoted in the 1930s by the Federal Housing Administration for lenders wanting to buy mortgage credit insurance. In Peru, Fondo MiVivienda is promoting standards for mortgage lending by making them a requirement for accessing its new financial products (mainly partial credit default insurance), designed in close collaboration with the industry.

High-quality servicing and collection. Investors in mortgage securities depend on originators and managers of special-purpose vehicles to ensure smooth collection, remit payments, and deal with arrears. A secondary mortgage market is more likely to develop—and the relative cost of funds is likely to be lower—if investors have confidence in the ability of issuers to perform this function, with remote monitoring of the manager of the special-purpose vehicle. In Mexico and many other countries, rating agencies assess the quality of mortgage servicers. Investors will require lower yields for mortgage-related securities that boast a highly rated servicer.

Professional standards of property appraisal. Investors must be confident in the value of the collateral underlying the lien. International best practices exist for property appraisals, promulgated by the International Valuation Standards Committee. Mexico's Sociedad Hipotecaria Federal promulgated appraisal standards for the loans that it either funds through its liquidity window or insures under its mortgage default insurance product.

The role of government. Government has an enabling role in primary real estate markets and in primary and secondary mortgage markets. National governments can work with local authorities to speed the registration and transfer of titles, to make urban land available for development, and to ensure sound construction practices to reduce the impact of natural disasters. National governments can balance the rights of creditors and debtors by requiring clear disclosures of loan terms and by simplifying and shortening foreclosure processes. As mentioned earlier, government reforms in Colombia and Mexico sharply reduced the time to foreclosure, and in Mexico, they gave lenders the option of using trust deeds to reduce the time even further.

Government should remove laws, taxes, and regulations that preclude or disadvantage mortgage securities, and regulatory regimes should reflect the safety that pledged mortgage securities can provide. For example, Chile removed stamp duties on securities registration. Issues of mortgage-backed securities grew, enabling banks to better tailor loan products for consumers and investment instruments for insurers and pension funds. Conversely, securitization has not been established in India, where stamp taxes in some states are as high as 12 percent. The requirement that borrowers consent to a transfer of ownership adds to the cost and hinders mortgage securitization. The trade tax in Germany has been a significant obstacle to securitization.

It is particularly important for legislators and regulators to create sound and thorough guidelines for the creation and bankruptcy remoteness of special-purpose vehicles and mortgage bonds. Securitization requires that the special-purpose vehicle have full rights over transferred assets and the proceeds from their liquidation, as well as the decision to liquidate them. Mortgage bond investors must have indisputable priority rights to the collateral, which should not be part of the general bankruptcy estate in the event of the issuer's bankruptcy, and ideally a priority right over the residual assets of the bankrupt entity if the cover pool is insufficient.

Many countries have public institutions to stimulate mortgage lending by mitigating liquidity risk, cash flow risk, and credit risk.[13] A few have been successful, but several have failed as a result of poor financial management. Two major causes are below-market pricing, necessitating repeated recapitalizations, and an inability (or politically driven unwillingness) to enforce the lien on defaulting loans. If the government creates such an institution, it should be run on commercial terms and focus on second-tier lending, with market-based pricing, reserving, and capital requirements. When considering such involvement, a government should ask several questions:

- Does the demand for government involvement reflect the nonexistence of or limited capacity for private market solutions (such as mortgage insurance, payment guarantees by private financial institutions) or simply a lender desire for cheaper financing that is unlikely to increase the flow of funds to housing?

- Can a public institution or guarantee program effectively manage and price risks? Will it have the incentives, autonomy, and capital to operate effectively without creating a large contingent liability for government?
- Once a public institution is created, is there a mechanism for eventual privatization or sunset, so that the government does not crowd out the private sector?
- Is there a clear and narrowly defined mission with clear accountability for the managers of the institution?

Although both economic and political reasons exist for government to stimulate mortgage capital markets, such involvement comes at a cost. Shifting risk to the government creates additional costs to monitor beneficiary agents, to reduce the potential for excessively risky lending and adverse selection. Government guarantees may be mispriced for political reasons, and government-supported institutions can exploit their monopoly. The costs and benefits of interventions need to be carefully weighed.

Government-sponsored or centralized private sector facilities that operate on market terms can shorten the learning curve for developing mortgage securities markets and provide the ancillary elements for their success. For example, individual Colombian banks issued their own mortgage-backed securities during the 1990s, but it took the scale economies and financial strength of the privately owned Titularizadora Colombiana to provide guaranteed, regular, and sizable issuances that could gain the required rating to make them attractive to investors.[14] Likewise, in Mexico, all 11 issues of mortgage-backed securities in the past four years benefited from credit enhancements, several from timely payment guarantees from Sociedad Hipotecaria Federal, the government's second-tier bank and guarantee facility.

Through its liquidity and mortgage default insurance products, Sociedad Hipotecaria Federal has promulgated standards for mortgage design and documentation. It originally catalyzed the primary market by funding mortgage SOFOLs when banks were all but absent from the origination market. Now, several of those SOFOLs have grown large enough to issue their own securities.

In Peru, Fondo MiVivienda has led the way to develop loan origination and documentation standards as part of the redesign of its funding and guarantee products. It provides incentives for banks to lend to lower-income segments of the population than in the past. Fondo MiVivienda has driven 40 percent of the recent growth in mortgage lending in Peru, funding more than 9,000 loans totaling US$213.3 million in 2005. Its keystone product is a combined line of credit, mortgage default insurance, and subsidy for timely borrower payment. As part of its efforts to develop mortgage securitization using its credit enhancements, Fondo MiVivienda has worked with the banking industry to develop standards for loan product design, origination, and documentation that will improve market efficiency. In addition, it will increasingly offer standalone guarantees without funding, which may in the medium term motivate mortgage originators to securitize part of their portfolios to reduce asset-liability mismatches.

Notes

1. Law 546 of 1999.

2. A caveat on these benefits is that in many cases, Colombian banks either retained some of the first loss tranches or bought back a significant percentage of the securitized mortgages to benefit from the advantageous tax exemption on yields.

3. A repurchase agreement is the sale of a security with a commitment by the seller to buy the security back (repurchase it) at a specified price at a specified later date.

4. As domestic interest rate derivatives products develop, investors should be able to partially hedge against the uncertainty created by the repayment option in the hands of the homeowners.

5. This was the case in the United States in the 1980s and in Mexico in the 1990s.

6. Bank investors in mortgage securities also benefit from the exemption of interest earned on the securities from income tax.

7. So, they would need to originate a joint multi-originator securitization bond.

8. The Colombian case is peculiar since the tax exemption on yields is appealing to banks and other potential investors, pushing yields down, while it has no value to tax-exempt pension funds, thus limiting their demand for mortgage-backed securities.

9. In 2002, public sector domestic bonds outstanding were about 17 percent of GDP in five large Latin American economies, compared with 10 percent for private sector bonds (de la Torre and Schmukler 2004).

10. In Guatemala, banks originate mortgages and then transform them into tradable bonds—*cedulas hipotecarias*—to benefit from the tax exemption on

interest earned on holding the *cedulas* and the reduced capital risk weight that results from default insurance.

11. Bankruptcy remoteness means that collateral backing securities or mortgage bond assets will remain out of the reach of other creditors in case of issuer insolvency.

12. Ley General de Bancos, articles 92, 99, and 113.

13. Liquidity risk refers to the risk that money will be needed before it is due. It can arise as a result of long-term mortgage loans. Individual mortgages may not be readily marketable (converted into cash). A lender faced with short-term and unstable sources of funds (deposits, short-term bank loans) may not offer mortgages because of the risk that it cannot meet cash outflow needs by selling its loans. Illiquid assets that cannot be pledged as collateral for short-term borrowing also increase liquidity risk.

14. Titularizadora Colombiana is owned by the mortgage lenders and by the International Finance Corporation, the private sector lending arm of the World Bank. It has no support from the state.

References

Buckley, Robert M., and Jerry Kalarickal, eds. 2006. *Thirty Years of World Bank Shelter Lending, What Have We Learned?* Washington, DC.: World Bank.

Caskey, John P., Celemente Ruiz Duran, and Tova Maria Solo. 2006. "The Urban Unbanked in Mexico and the United States." Policy Research Working Paper 3835, World Bank, Washington, DC.

Chiquier, Loic, Olivier Hassler, and Michael Lea. 2004. "Mortgage Securities in Emerging Markets." Policy Research Working Paper 3370, World Bank, Washington, DC.

de la Torre, Augusto, and Sergio Schmukler. 2004. "Whither Latin American Capital Markets?" World Bank, Washington, DC.

Fitch Ratings. 2005. "Estrés de Prepagos—lecciones y perspectivas futuras." New York.

Jappelli, Tullio, Marco Pagano, and Magda Bianco. 2002. "Courts and Banks: Effects of Judicial Enforcement on Credit Markets." Centre for Studies in Economics and Finance Working Paper 58. Università degli Studi di Salerno, Dipartimento di Scienze Economiche.

Pence, Karen M. 2003. "Foreclosing on Opportunity: State Laws and Mortgage Credit." Board of Governors of the Federal Reserve System, Washington, DC.

Renaud, Bertrand. 1987. "Another Look at Housing Finance in Developing Countries." *Cities* 4 (1): 28–34.

SBIF (Superintendencia de Bancos e Instituciones Financieras de Chile). 2006. "Serie Técnica de Estudios No. 004." Santiago.

Solo, Tova Maria, and Astrid Manroth. 2006. "Access to Financial Services in Colombia." Policy Research Working Paper 3834, World Bank, Washington, DC.

Titularizadora Colombiana. 2005. "Financiación de vivienda y titularización hipotecaria en Latinoamérica." Bogotá.

CHAPTER 3

Structured Finance for Infrastructure

Some studies project that infrastructure investment needs in developing countries over 2005–10 will reach US$465 billion annually, with US$71 billion of that in Latin America. These needs will be driven by repair and rehabilitation, compliance with environmental standards, coverage of the existing population, and projected increases in population. Transport is projected to account for 39 percent of investment needs, energy (electricity and power) for 38 percent, water and sanitation for 12 percent, and telecommunications for 11 percent.

In many countries, a shift is expected toward investment by subnational entities. It is estimated that the share of subsovereign needs may average 85 percent in water and sewerage, 60 percent in transport, 50 percent in energy, and 10 percent in telecommunications (Noel and Sirtaine forthcoming). Based on these estimates and available data on sectoral shares, required subsovereign infrastructure investments across Latin America are estimated at US$38 billion annually over 2005–10.

Financing is of prime importance, especially since central governments generally have very limited fiscal headroom. Can the private sector finance most of these investments? Under what conditions? Could it also finance often smaller and riskier municipal and regional projects? If not, what alternative sources of funding can be tapped? Could the capital markets

Figure 3.1.   Expected Annual Investment Needs in Infrastructure in Emerging Markets
(2005–10)

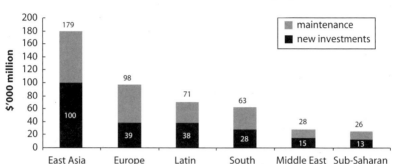

Total annual investment needs in developing countries

Source: Fay and Yepes (2003).

Note: The authors estimate demand for infrastructure services over the first decade of the new millennium based on a model that relates demand for infrastructure with the structural change and growth in income the world is expected to undergo between now and 2010. It should be noted that predictions are based on estimated demand rather than on any absolute measure of "need" such as those developed in the Millennium Development Goals. The authors also provide estimates of associated investment and maintenance expenditures and predict total required resource flows to satisfy new demand while maintaining service for existing infrastructure. Infrastructure includes roads, railroads, telecommunications, electricity, water, and sanitation. The GDP deflator used is an average of the 2005–10 projections.

play a larger role? Under what conditions? What could be the role of local institutional investors in countries that underwent pension system reforms? These are the main questions this chapter investigates.

Why Infrastructure Financing Has Dried Up

Until the late 1980s, governments were the main source of infrastructure financing in Latin America. They raised funds through ordinary revenues, earmarked taxes, or borrowing on their own account through loans or bonds issued as general sovereign debt.

In the 1990s, governments mostly had to abandon public provision of infrastructure. They lacked the fiscal resources to continue supporting loss-making and inefficient public service providers. In addition, they faced competing demands for resources—from expenditures on social services, for example. So, governments sought private sector participation. This helped governments reconcile the large infrastructure investment needs and the limited space for government borrowing. Governments also hoped for efficiency gains from private management and control of investment decisions. With these benefits in mind, infrastructure policies in much of the 1990s assumed that financing would shift from its traditional sources—the public sector and international aid—toward the private sector.

Across developing countries, private participation in infrastructure increased rapidly, from US$18 billion in 1990 to a peak of US$110 billion in 1997. But it declined to US$55 billion in 2003 (its 1995 level). It has risen slightly since, but experts agree that it will take many years to return to its peak, if it ever does.

Latin America and the Caribbean have led in private participation in infrastructure, with the private sector contributing 47 percent of investments done over 1990–2004. East Asia and the Pacific had private investments of 24 percent and Europe and Central Asia, 15 percent. The Latin America and the Caribbean region pioneered opening infrastructure to private participation, with reasonably high growth, overall macroeconomic stability, and a gradual shift toward greater, more open economies.

But Latin America was not spared the radical global fall in private participation in infrastructure at the end of the 1990s. Private participation in Latin America fell from US$65 billion in 1998 to US$15 billion in 2003 and US$17 billion in 2004. Estimated annual needs over the next five years are US$71 billion (US$355 billion), nearly as much as Latin America attracted over the last 15 years (US$375 billion).

In recent years, many private investors have lost their appetite for infrastructure projects in Latin America (and in developing countries in general). The main factors:

- Greater macroeconomic instability.
- Growing public discontent over privatizations and contractual terminations.
- Rising investor concerns over inapplicable contractual agreements and weak regulators and regulatory frameworks.

Severe constraints limit the capacity of national and subnational governments to finance their growing infrastructure needs. First, central governments often face fiscal constraints. Only a few countries in Latin America (such as Chile) have low public indebtedness that leaves room for public sector borrowing to finance infrastructure investments.[1] Second, local and regional governments—expected to initiate a significant part of future infrastructure investments—are hampered by deficiencies in the subnational finance market. The legal and regulatory frameworks for subnational bond issues are weak, as is market infrastructure. Obstacles hinder access to the financial markets for infrastructure financing, including weak fiscal decentralization frameworks and lack of capacity and experience in complex infrastructure projects. The playing field is uneven, and too few subnational bond enhancement instruments help governments reach a level of creditworthiness that could appeal to institutional investors.

Public-Private Partnerships for Infrastructure Financing

Many infrastructure investments are brought to the private sector as concessions (or similar contracts) and financed through project finance arrangements, generally without recourse to the project sponsors. So, if the project company goes bankrupt, its creditors have limited claim on the assets of the project company's shareholders. Lending is provided against only the anticipated cash flows of the project, with no (or very limited) recourse to the project sponsors. The infrastructure project or concession is like a complex special-purpose vehicle. Private lenders will thus carefully gauge the risks of the projects against the expected return. The limited role of capital markets in infrastructure financing—and the critical role of financial engineering through pledges and securities to attract capital market financing—reflects the inability of many infrastructure investments to offer an attractive risk-return balance, at least without significant credit enhancements.

Despite private investors' willingness to accept greater risks to achieve greater returns or diversification, they have often avoided certain risks (table 3.1). In general, private investors have:

- Assumed construction, operational, commercial, and financial risks.
- Insured against *"force majeure"* and political risks.
- Used the project's contractual arrangements (or sometimes guarantees) to protect against regulatory and exchange rate risks—and favor projects able to raise local currency financing.

To ensure protection against the last two categories of risk, investors have often required that appropriate instruments, such as insurance or guarantees, shift the recourse of lenders to guarantors, the host government, or other third parties.[2]

Table 3.1. Typical Risk Allocation among Project Participants

Risk	Example of risk	Group traditionally bearing risk	Instrument to allocate risk
Construction	Construction cost overrun or delay	Private sector	Project contract
Operational	Operational cost overrun or sub-standard operational performance	Private sector	Project contract
"Force majeure"	Natural disaster	Private sector	Insurance, project contract
Commercial	Insufficient demand, private supplier or purchaser contracts not honored	Private sector (or host country in part)	Project contract (sometimes minimum revenue guarantee)
Financial	Interest rate fluctuations, funding uncertainties	Private sector	Project contract, financial structuring
Political	Expropriation, revocation of permits, asset confiscation, currency inconvertibility or nontransferability, war, riots	Host country or third-party guarantor	Political risk guarantee or insurance
Regulatory	Changes in laws and regulations, tariff-setting rules, taxation, public supplier or purchaser contracts not honored	Host country or third-party guarantor	Project contract, partial risk guarantee
Exchange rate	Risk of currency devaluation or depreciation	Host country (sometimes private sector)	Project contract, foreign exchange guarantee, or structured financing

The Role of Guarantees in Infrastructure Financing

The use of government guarantees may not be sufficient for investors. When the risks that private lenders and investors do not want to bear are taken up by the host government (through government guarantees to the project company), lenders and investors become exposed to the host government, and the credit rating of the project is linked to that of the country. This may be insufficient for international lenders—and even for local investors who are overexposed to the sovereign government. Indeed, in many Latin American countries, the pension funds and insurance companies, among the largest institutional investors, are invested mostly in government securities. Shifting project risks to the government would thus further increase their exposure to the government.

Guarantees from third parties, such as multilateral institutions or specialized financial risk monoline insurers, are sometimes needed. Allowing the projects' credit rating to exceed the country's limit and shifting exposure to outside parties, such instruments can make projects attractive to investors. This explains why—even in an investment-grade country such as Chile— third-party guarantees have been required to cover certain project risks. The credibility of a guarantee depends on the perceived creditworthiness of the guarantor to meet guarantee payment claims. Because guarantees can allocate risks to those who best control them, they reduce the probability that these risks happen—and therefore carry the additional advantage of reducing the cost and increasing the maturity of the guaranteed funds.[3]

But guarantees are not a panacea. First, risk mitigation techniques can help mobilize private savings, but they cannot alone make a poorly conceived project economically and financially viable. Second, guarantees do not overcome one of the main obstacles to project development in developing countries: the lack of institutional capacity of national or subnational authorities to develop financially attractive projects and implement them in a timely manner. Third, guarantees may not be sufficient to enable infrastructure projects to raise money on the capital markets, even if their rating becomes high enough. They have some inherent features, such as excessive risk during construction, that make them unattractive for private capital market financing up front.

The Capital Markets: An Alternative Source of Financing for Infrastructure?

In this changing environment, Latin American countries—like many other emerging countries—are facing a dilemma. Their infrastructure investment needs are expected to grow well above historical trends as a result of maintenance requirements, tougher environmental standards, and pressure to expand coverage, especially in poorer areas. But private participation in infrastructure has hovered at a low level, and public financing sources remain limited.

Policymakers are thus seeking alternative sources of funding that could bridge the gap. The capital markets seem to be an obvious source, given the large funds of institutional investors, especially the pension funds. Pension funds' total assets exceeded US$300 billion in Latin America in 2005, four times the estimated infrastructure investment needs of US$70 billion a year (table 3.2). And from September 2004 to September 2005, pension fund investment portfolios grew by about US$80 billion.

Capital markets have historically provided very little funding to infrastructure projects. In concessions across the world, the vast majority of debt has come from syndicated bank loans, with capital market bonds playing a minor role.

The use of bond issues in infrastructure was abysmal until 1998, when it seems to have taken off (figure 3.2). But the observed growth is largely attributable to telecommunications companies, accounting for 50–70 percent of the value of all issues over 1998–2001. In addition, about 94 percent of these infrastructure bonds were issued by companies in developed markets, with only 6 percent in emerging markets. The stock market crash of 2001 and investor concerns about private infrastructure participation are likely to have led to a significant slowdown in infrastructure bond issues after 2001.

A strikingly low number of infrastructure companies access the bond market in Latin America, and these generally require credit enhancements. Chile is often cited as having tapped the capital market to finance infrastructure investments. But most of the bonds originated from established energy corporations, with very few issues by project companies. When Chilean project companies attracted significant capital market participation, as in the transport sector, they generally benefited from sub-

Table 3.2. Total Investment Portfolios of Latin American Pension Funds

Countries	Funds (US$ million)	
	9/30/2005	9/30/2004
Mandatory systems		
Argentina	22,835	17,065
Bolivia	1,871	1,670
Colombia	14,749	9,312
Costa Rica	686	484
Chile	72,500	52,718
El Salvador	2,780	1,982
Mexico	56,568	39,220
Peru	9,690	7,253
Dominican Republic	328	127
Uruguay	2,064	1,499
Total	184,071	131,330
Voluntary systems		
Brazil: Abrapp	116,038	82,390
Anapp	18,769	21,417
Honduras	187	9
Total	134,825	103,816
Overall total	318,896	235,146

Source: International Federation of Pension Fund Administrators.

Note: Abrapp: Brazilian Pension Funds Association; Anapp: National Association of Private Social Security.

Figure 3.2. Trends in Bonds Issued to Finance Infrastructure Projects

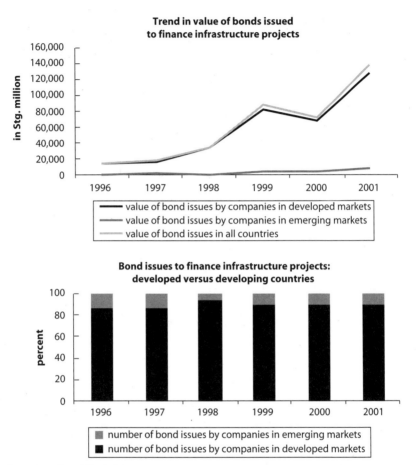

Source: Alexander and Chia (2002).

stantial structured financing, through guarantees and other protections (box 3.1). The importance of covenants for infrastructure bonds is confirmed in a global study showing that about 70 percent of all infrastructure bonds benefited from some enhancement (figure 3.3).

While bond financing has some key advantages over loan financing, it may not always have the needed flexibility for project financing. Capital market debt is usually offered with longer maturities than bank loans, better matching the duration of infrastructure investments. In addition, interest rates on infrastructure bonds tend to be fixed rather than floating, limiting exposure

Box 3.1

Infrastructure Bonds in Chile

Many of Chile's transport concessions raised a large part of their financing from the local capital market. From 1996 to 2003, infrastructure bonds issued in Chile averaged about US$1 billion a year and accounted for more than half the country's total bond issues. Most of the bonds issued, however, originated from established energy corporations, with very few issues by project companies. When Chilean project companies attracted significant capital market participation, they generally benefited from a government minimum revenue guarantee and, in some cases, a foreign exchange guarantee, limiting significantly the risks borne by bondholders. In addition, political and regulatory risks were insured in nearly all cases by the Inter-American Development Bank or private insurers.

Road concessions with public bond issues	Road insurance?	Minimum revenue guarantee?	Foreign exchange guarantee?
Autopista del Sol	Yes	Yes	No
Talca Chilian	Yes	Yes	No
Autopista Los Libertadores	Yes	Yes	No
Autopista del Bosque	Yes	Yes	No
Ruta de la Araucania	Yes	N.A.	N.A.
Rutas del Pacificos	Yes	No	No
Autopista del Maipú	N.A.	Yes	Yes
Melipilla	No	Yes	No
Autopista Central	Yes	Yes	No
Costanera Norte	Yes	Yes	Yes

Source: Government of Chile.

to interest rate risk. But a bond issue gives the borrower less flexibility, especially in providing tailored structures, matching repayments with construction financing needs, or obtaining a grace period during construction.

So, capital market financing seems better suited to finance utilities or to refinance project debt after the construction phase rather than to provide initial financing to greenfield projects. Historical data seem to confirm this conclusion, since capital market investments in infrastructure have focused on established companies in the telecommunications sector, where construction risk is usually the lowest.

Figure 3.3. Covenants on Infrastructure Bonds

Covenants by volume of issues

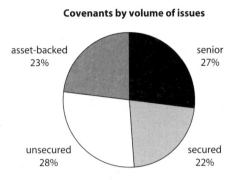

asset-backed
23%

senior
27%

unsecured
28%

secured
22%

Source: Dailami (2004).

Pension Fund Regulation and Infrastructure Investments

Another constraint on the participation of capital market investors in financing infrastructure projects is the regulations governing the investments of pension funds and other institutional investors. Because funds have a fiduciary responsibility, their investment activities tend to be regulated. This is particularly true for pension funds, which invest old-age savings. Regulations usually cover the range of permissible investments; their liquidity in terms of a reference for marking to market; their mandatory risk rating, valuation, and risk characteristics; and the portfolio, such as requiring some minimum return. Some of these regulations severely constrain the ability of pension funds to invest in infrastructure securities, as discussed in chapter 1.

Pension funds often face regulatory limitations to investing in infrastructure bonds. As Latin American countries began to sell infrastructure assets to private investors in the beginning of the 1990s, some governments modified pension fund regulations to allow them to invest conservatively in infrastructure stocks and bonds. But today only a few Latin American countries explicitly allow investments in infrastructure (including greenfield projects): Chile, Argentina, Colombia, and Peru. Even in these countries, restrictions and limits apply to pension fund investments in infrastructure. As a result, the share of pension fund assets invested in infrastructure in Latin America is small, though it has grown somewhat recently, typically through structured financing solutions. The investment in infrastructure bonds is often reported as part of corporate sector financing, which may underestimate the involvement of pension funds in infrastructure (table 3.3).

Table 3.3. Breakdown of Pension Fund Investment Portfolios in Latin America
(percent)

	Government bonds	Corporate sector	Financial sector	Foreign investments	Other assets	Total investments	Liquid assets	Total
Argentina	62	15	12	10	0	98	2	100
Bolivia	67	24	6	1	0	99	1	100
Colombia	49	20	21	10	1	100	0	100
Costa Rica								
Chile	19	24	30	27	0	100	0	100
El Salvador	84	0	10	6	0	100	0	100
Mexico	85	14	0	0	0	99	1	100
Peru	27	37	27	8	0	100	0	100
Dominican Republic	0	0	100	0	0	100	0	100
Uruguay	79	5	7	0	0	92	8	100

Source: International Federation of Pension Fund Administrators.

It is unclear how much relaxing the regulatory limits would increase infrastructure investments. Some argue that, if pension fund regulations were relaxed, pension funds would invest more in infrastructure, because good-quality infrastructure assets would provide diversification opportunities and possibly a higher return. But infrastructure investments, especially in greenfield projects, are inherently risky, so any changes in regulations would be gradual and gauged carefully by pension funds. In the meantime, attracting higher pension fund investment in infrastructure will require adapting instruments offered to pension funds to the existing regulations, generally including substantial risk protection. As a reference, most Organisation for Economic Co-operation and Development countries apply a prudent investor rule to guide pension fund investments, leaving more freedom to invest in infrastructure.

Further Mobilizing Private Capital

To attract private project sponsors and financiers, the design and financing of projects must be structured to reduce overall exposure to uncontrollable risks. In particular:

- To minimize currency exposure, investors are likely to favor projects with a large share of local currency financing or adequate protection against foreign exchange risk.
- To minimize political and regulatory risks and exposure to the sovereign, they are likely to require that government undertakings are backstopped, when necessary, by multilateral agencies or other third parties.

Various project structuring methods have been used in Latin America to attract private investors and mobilize private capital in infrastructure projects. They can be broadly categorized as:

- Mechanisms directly reducing the project's risks or improving its resilience to shocks—to attract project sponsors.
- Mechanisms limiting exposure to project risks—to attract lenders.

The trend is toward increasingly complex contractual structures. As a result, capacity to develop viable project structures also must be enhanced, particularly for local and national authorities in emerging markets.

For Project Sponsors—Mechanisms Directly Reducing Project Risks

To reduce projects' vulnerability to external shocks, mechanisms are needed to raise local currency financing or set up liquidity facilities for contingencies. In Latin American countries with well-developed local currency yield curves and long-term cross-currency swaps,[4] projects can benefit from local currency financing from international lenders. Multilateral institutions started to offer local currency loans in countries where long-dated currency risk hedging is possible or where they can raise funds to match their exposure (box 3.2). Governments can also facilitate the access of private projects to such financing by negotiating local currency credit lines with multilateral institutions that could be on-lent to provide local currency financing to infrastructure projects through development or commercial banks.

When local currency financing is not available, contingent liquidity facilities linked to exchange rate movements can help achieve the credit enhancement to attract private project financiers and institutional investors. For instance, in 2001, the Overseas Private Investment Corporation (OPIC) developed a liquidity facility structure to protect infrastructure bonds against foreign exchange risks in an energy distribution project in Brazil (the AES Tiête project). The structure provided a revolving liq-

---

Box 3.2

IFC Local Currency Loan in Mexico

The International Finance Corporation (IFC), part of the World Bank Group, offers local currency loans to infrastructure projects in Latin American countries where it can fully hedge its foreign exchange exposure to dollars in the currency swap market. For example, in 2003, the Mexican private water and sewerage company, Compañía Tratadora de Aguas Negras de Puerto Vallarta, obtained a peso-denominated loan from the IFC (equivalent to US$7million) to build and operate a municipal wastewater treatment plant. The company undertook this project on a build-own-transfer (BOT) basis under a 15-year contract with the water authority of Puerto Vallarta. Because revenues are earned in local currency, the loan—denominated in local currency and with a fixed interest rate—enabled the company to minimize currency mismatches and interest rate risk. By reducing the project's risk profile, it helped attract private investors, even though the project was one of the first BOT wastewater projects by the private sector.

uidity credit line to the project company if it reached high default risk on debt obligations due to fluctuations in the bilateral exchange rate between the Brazilian real and the dollar. A US$30 million foreign exchange liquidity facility supported US$300 million in financing (box 3.3). Similar liquidity facilities could be put in place with the help of multilaterals.

Such structures may not work in cases of extreme foreign exchange shocks. In Argentina in 2001, providing liquidity to a project company would have allowed it to continue operating despite the adverse conditions. But if tariffs are not ultimately adjusted to the new exchange rate, the project company will still not be able to repay its loans.

Liquidity facilities and (contingent) credit lines can also protect against other risks. These facilities often take the form of credit lines the project company can tap during financial difficulties, either freely or contingent on some event. An example is Financiera del Desarrollo Territorial in Colombia, established in 1989 by the government of Colombia with World Bank support as a second-tier bank for local government financing. It developed instruments to support private infrastructure projects, facilitating financing in the domestic and international markets, including a facility supporting liquidity against government payment delays.

Box 3.3

OPIC Liquidity Facility

The liquidity facility works as a contingent source of funding triggered by foreign exchange shock. It makes a revolving credit line available to the project company if a depreciation of the Brazilian real prevents the issuer from meeting its debt service obligations. The liquidity facility is triggered when the borrower's revenues, converted to dollars, are below the floor value and insufficient for payment of scheduled debt service (see box figure).

The claim is paid through a loan subordinated only to the project's senior lenders, with an interest rate reflecting the subordinated nature of the claim. Coverage is structured to isolate currency risks from operational risks. Senior lenders remain exposed to all operational risks. A pro forma calculation is performed to determine how much the revenue shortfall is due to fluctuations in currency values (enabling a claim under the devaluation coverage) and how much is due to negative operational results (and no claim is possible under the devaluation coverage).

Box 3.3 (*continued*)

The structure was received well by rating agencies and institutional investors. The company became the first electric power project to achieve an investment-grade rating in a below-investment-grade country, its bond issue obtained the longest tenor ever by a Brazilian corporate issuer, and it was priced at a level equivalent to 237 basis points fewer than Brazilian sovereign debt. This is evidence that it was perceived as less risky than other investments in the country, indicating that credit analysts believed that the project had been largely isolated from Brazilian macroeconomic risk.

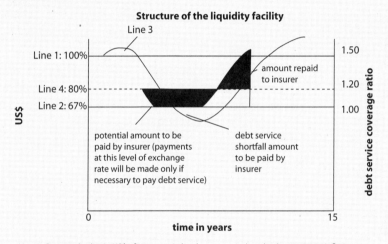

Line 1: Projected value in US$ of revenues in local currency, indexed to host country inflation rate
Line 2: Annual debt service requirements in US$ (principal and interest)
Line 3: Actual value in US$ of revenues in local currency, indexed to host country inflation rate
Line 4: A line showing the level of revenues at which the project has a debt service ratio of 1.2

Source: OPIC.

For Lenders—Mechanisms Limiting Exposure to Project or Subnational Risks

Lenders to infrastructure projects finance either a standalone project or a subsovereign entity. In both cases, bond issuance will require credit enhancements through securitization, partial guarantees, or setting up infrastructure funds.

Standalone projects. Securitization structures are used to bypass the creditworthiness of primary issuers and rely instead on the credit rating of the underlying project assets or flows. Utilities around the world are relying more on securitizing future income flows to back up bond issues.

Latin American domestic securitizations of future flows are estimated at US$2.7 billion in 2005, mostly for utilities and energy companies and primarily purchased by domestic pension funds. Introduced in Brazil in 2004, infrastructure securitizations were 20 percent of Brazilian domestic securitization volume in 2005, with three transactions totaling US$700 million, mainly by power distribution and generation companies, as well as a first future flow oil royalties securitization. In Mexico in 2005, five tranches of future flow deals totaled more than US$1 billion, mostly by the electricity company. Further growth in such structures is expected in 2006. Similar transactions occurred in Peru, Colombia, and Uruguay (box 3.4). Historically, the Panama and El Salvador markets have been driven partly by future flows transactions, but they have been quiet recently (a large Panama Sur project is in the pipeline). In Argentina in 2006, Fitch expects the debut of securitizations for infrastructure improvements in electricity and gas, forecasting continued growth of future flow securitizations for infrastructure companies.

Box 3.4

Administración Nacional de Usinas y Transmisiones Eléctricas (UTE)—June 2005 Bond Issue

UTE raised US$25 million on the local market in June 2005. The bonds achieved a AA+ local rating and were more than three times oversubscribed. They are structured through the securitization in a special purpose vehicle of UTE's future electricity revenues, collected by an independent agent.

The characteristics of the bonds:

- Amount: US$25 million.
- Maturity: 7 years.
- Interest payment: London interbank offered rate + 3 percent, with a floor of 6.5 percent and a ceiling of 8.5 percent.
- Amortization: equal biannual payments.
- Rating: AA+, by Fitch Ratings.
- Enhancement: securitization of future electricity revenues (current revenues of US$500 million equivalent).
- Company revenues administered by a trustee.

Securitization has been used little in concessions and greenfield projects, but these may be growth areas for structured bonds, mainly in response to the appetite of domestic institutional investors. In standalone infrastructure projects, securitization is used mostly to raise cheap refinancing after construction and initial startup. For example, toll road structured bonds totaled US$400 million in Mexico in 2005. It could be argued that project financing is a project-wide securitization, since financing is normally provided on the basis of future project flows.

In Peru, securitization was part of the structure to raise bond financing in the early stages of concessions. Access to the Camisea gas field was given as a concession in 2004 to a special-purpose company, Transportadora de Gas del Peru. Various international companies sponsored the project. In 2004 and 2005, the company raised US$350 million equivalent through four issuances of domestic securitization bonds of future flows, the majority purchased by domestic pension funds. Interestingly, one of these bonds was inflation indexed and largely subscribed by life insurance companies (annuity providers).

Private bond insurance and partial guarantees can also provide the required risk protection and credit enhancement. These can be blanket guarantees (also called full credit guarantees)—to protect against debt default, regardless of the cause—or partial risk guarantees to protect against specific risks, sometimes used in addition to securitization to provide a residual credit enhancement. For example, most Chilean infrastructure bonds issued by road concession companies were covered by private guarantees. Private sector guarantors, called "monoline" in the capital markets (MBIA, AMBAC, XL Capital Assurance, CIFG, and so on, all rated AAA), can provide financial guarantees on bond issues (generally blanket guarantees). But they normally require that the transaction be investment grade internationally. So, they are mostly active in investment-grade countries or in future flow transactions in which offshore receivables underpin debt service and in which the sovereign rating can, in effect, be exceeded. Monoliner credit enhancement typically brings the debt issuance to international AAA rating, which may be too expensive and not necessary to attract domestic institutional investors, typically content with AAA or AA domestic ratings. Some private sector guarantors (commonly called "multilines") do not require the underlying transaction to be rated investment grade, but their activity in Latin America has been very limited and their interest in financial guarantees has fallen.

Partial risk guarantees or other similar guarantees from specialized political insurers or multilateral institutions can give adequate protection to lenders while shifting their exposure to the multilateral institution providing the guarantee. The risk coverage of each guarantee is tailored to the specific transaction. The risks that can be covered include risks related to tariffs, the regulatory framework, rights of way, licenses, expropriations, termination amounts, interferences in arbitration processes, the rule of law, convertibility and transferability, and subsidy payments. In general, the efficient allocation of risks that partial risk guarantees allow has a strong positive impact on project financing, increasing maturity and decreasing cost. In addition, when multilateral and bilateral guarantors fill the investment-grade gap, the capacity of private guarantors to offer partial or full credit guarantees can be enhanced significantly (box 3.5). The Multilateral Investment Guarantee Agency, part of the World Bank Group, provides political risk (especially breach of contract) insurance to enhance the potential for private sector financing. In a transaction in the Dominican Republic in 2006, a greenfield concession to build a toll road was financed largely through a US$160 million bond, which received a credit enhancement through the agency's 51 percent guarantee of outstanding bonds.

Another option is using infrastructure funds to raise financing in the local or international financial markets in lieu of small project companies. The funds have usually received some initial capitalization from the government, investments banks with high credit ratings, or donors and used it as a reserve fund (or seed capital) to secure subsequent bond issues to fund infrastructure projects. Credit quality is enhanced for bond investors thanks to the reserve fund, the diversification effect of investments in several projects, and the credit rating of the fund's shareholders. Indeed, these funds, usually set up as special-purpose vehicles, often enjoy some guarantee from their highly rated shareholders. The Fondo de Rotación (Revolving Fund), set up by the government of Colombia, raised financing from the local capital market for on-lending to water companies for water and sewerage investment projects. A special-purpose vehicle, it received initial seed capital from a loan from the Inter-American Development Bank and subsequent capital infusions from the Ministry of Finance (which may indicate some fiscal risk in such a vehicle). It used the capital to support bonds issued in the capital markets. Another example is the infrastructure investment fund of the Mexican development bank Banobras, which provides contingent funding to support commercial debt issued during construction. The experience with infrastructure funds is mixed, however, with problems relating mostly to faulty design (in objectives, instruments, pricing, and sectors targeted) and poor management.

Box 3.5

Sociedad Acueducto, Alcantarillado y Aseo de Barranquilla Local Currency Inflation-Indexed Bond Issue, May 20, 2003

Sociedad Acueducto, Alcantarillado y Aseo de Barranquilla (Triple A) was awarded in a 20-year concession 1993, later extended to 2033, to provide water, sewerage, and solid waste services to Barranquilla, the fourth largest city in Colombia. As part of the concession, the company undertook the Suroccidente project to extend water and sewerage services to the southwest of Barranquilla, the poorest part of the city, connecting 350,000 low-income inhabitants to the network. These investments were first financed through short-term dollar debt, creating a substantial maturity and currency mismatch on the project company's balance sheet.

In 2003, Triple A sought an IFC credit enhancement to improve the credit rating of a proposed bond issue, to refinance and enable a bond maturity of up to 10 years in the local capital market. The enhancement was a partial credit guarantee of US$3 million, covering up to 25 percent of the principal amount of the bond issue (US$63 million equivalent). The bonds were rated AAA on the national scale, a three-notch increase over the company's rating. The issue, denominated in inflation-indexed local currency, was fully subscribed by more than 15 domestic institutional investors. It was the first bond issue by a Colombian corporation with a rating below AA, contributing to the development of Colombia's domestic capital market.

The bond characteristics:
- Amount: 180 billion Colombian pesos (approximately US$63 million).
- Maturity: 10 years.
- Interest payment: CPI + 8.5 percent, payable quarterly.
- Principal payment: equal annual payments over the last 5 years.
- Rating: coAAA by Duff and Phelp de Colombia and BRC Investor Services.
- Enhancement: IFC guarantee for the greater of five coupon payments, or 25 percent of the outstanding principal, up to US$18.24 million.
- Company revenues administered by a trustee.

Subnational infrastructure. Long-term efforts are needed to ensure that subnational entities have greater access to financial markets to finance their infrastructure investments. This requires improving fiscal decentralization frameworks, building the institutional capacity of subnational governments, strengthening governance, and undertaking regulatory and legal reforms. As these long-term reforms are being put in place, several mechanisms can facilitate subnational access to infrastructure bond markets. Typically aiming at limiting investors' exposure to subnational project risks, these mechanisms are similar to those used for large private projects discussed in the prior subsection.

Securitizing future tax revenues or federal transfers is the main way for low-rating subsovereigns to tap the bond market. Using the CB instrument, future federal tax securitizations—mainly issued by states—were a third of Mexico's securitizations in 2005. This class of securitization was more than 10 percent of Latin America's structured bonds in 2005.

Partial credit guarantees issued by private financial insurers or multilateral institutions can enhance bonds issued by subnational public entities. By reducing bondholders' risk exposure, partial credit guarantees make the bonds more attractive to investors, and generally have a strong positive impact on maturities and interest rates. Multilaterals are trying to develop complementary guarantee products for local government risk to be taken without counter-guarantees from the central government.

Partial credit guarantees can be offered through facilities to mainstream their accessibility by subsovereign issuers. Although no partial credit–guarantee facilities exist in Latin America, their applications in Asia and in Eastern Europe suggest their potential. Established in 1998 as a financial services corporation by 16 private member banks, the Local Government Unit Guarantee Corporation in the Philippines is a commercial entity that guarantees local government municipal bonds with a full credit guarantee covering principal and interest. It charges a fee to municipalities at the time of bond issue and draws on its reserves and reinsurance policies in case of default. If necessary, it can divert local revenue transfers to service a guarantee claim. Also a channel moving private capital into local government investments, the corporation is responsible for the Philippines' small but growing municipal bond market—in an economy otherwise dominated by the banking system. Most of the municipal bonds issued in the Philippines since 1998 have carried its guarantee.

A strong balance sheet for raising infrastructure bonds for subnational projects can be created by establishing an infrastructure fund with strong shareholders. In South Africa, the Infrastructure Finance Corporation Limited was established in 1996 with private capital and management to finance infrastructure backlogs. It issues bonds in the local and international capital markets, borrows long-term funds from international financial institutions, and on-lends to municipalities, water boards, and other

Box 3.6

Bond Issues for Tlalnepantla Municipal Water Conservation Project and the Vía Atlixcáyotl Toll Road in Mexico

The Tlalnepantla municipal water conservation project in Mexico is an example of the use of the World Bank Group's Municipal Fund guarantees to support a public-private partnership infrastructure project. The Municipal Fund and Dexia (a private bank) provided a partial credit guarantee for 90 percent of the principal of a 10-year bond issue in Mexican pesos for the equivalent of US$9.2 million. A trust was established to raise funds and on-lend to the Tlalnepantla Municipal Water Company and the municipality of Tlalnepantla as joint obligators to finance a wastewater treatment plant. The main financing objectives of the municipality were to better match the maturity of its debt with its long-term infrastructure investments and to access long-dated savings in the institutional investors market. The credit enhancement from the Municipal Fund and Dexia helped the bonds achieve a local rating of AAA, two levels above the municipality's standalone rating. Through this operation, the Municipal Fund supported the first municipal bond issue in Mexico without direct access to federal transfers. Most of the credit risk was taken over by the highly creditworthy guarantors.

The state of Puebla securitized the future flows of a toll road between Puebla and Atlixco. The 15-year domestic bond was about US$52 million + 6.5 percent, with increasing principal amortizations. It was subscribed mainly by pension funds and insurance companies. The state's toll roads are managed by Carreteras de Cuota Puebla, a public decentralized entity. An additional enhancement was a partial guarantee from Banobras (the local development bank), which helped it reach a mxAAA rating by Fitch and Standard & Poor's, higher than for the state of Puebla (mxA+) or the municipality of Puebla (mxAA−). This partial guarantee from Banobras was cheaper than an alternative monoline wrap and as effective in lowering the cost of funding, given that local investors do not seek international AAA ratings.

statutory institutions that establish social and economic infrastructure in South Africa. This funding has been mainly long-term loans with fixed interest rates. Maintaining an AA rating through careful project selection, the corporation is the second issuer of corporate bonds in South Africa and the main provider of financing for municipal infrastructure investments since 1997.

The Way Forward

Local currency financing instruments and political and regulatory risk guarantees are most likely to attract private corporate and institutional investors in infrastructure. Governments can facilitate access to these instruments by setting up dedicated structures, including infrastructure funds, liquidity facilities, credit lines, and well-designed guarantee facilities. They can also catalyze local currency financing by leading the way in local yield curve development, by having sensible investment and risk management regulations for domestic institutional investors, and by providing regulatory, taxation, and accounting practices conducive to sustainable development of currency and interest rate derivatives.

To facilitate the access to the capital market by subnational entities—expected to drive a higher share of infrastructure investments—credit enhancement instruments will also be needed. Multilateral institutions can enhance the credit rating of subnational entities, particularly by building subnational institutional capacity, providing subnational bond guarantees, and enabling subnational entities to tap the often large resources of domestic institutional investors—with or without central government support.

Even so, the constraints on bond financing mean that the capital markets are not likely to become a major source of infrastructure financing in emerging markets. Important constraints are the risk aversion of private investors in the current environment, the difficulty in structuring adequate risk-sharing mechanisms, the inherent unattractiveness of project structures for bond investments, and regulatory constraints on pension funds and other institutional investors. These explain why infrastructure bond financing has been so little used worldwide—and why it has been limited mostly to established corporations, chiefly in telecommunications, in a limited number of countries and with large protections for investors. But the capital markets, including pension funds, can play a large role in funding fundamentally sound and well-structured projects, with adequate risk-sharing agreements to allocate risks, provide security to institutional investors, and address external constraints.

Notes

1. These countries have a ratio of general government debt outstanding to GDP below 30 percent.

2. In countries with a well-developed local currency yield curve, currency derivatives tend to flourish if provided an adequate legal and institutional frame-

work, which can present international investors with appealing market-based hedging alternatives.

3. The reduction in cost and extension in maturities should not be considered a subsidy. They result from an overall reduction in project risks through the optimal allocation of risks that guarantees make possible.

4. In the countries where the local currency yield curve is well developed, financial intermediaries can typically structure long-dated currency swaps—for example, Mexico has a well-developed over-the-counter and organized exchange (MexDer) for interest rate futures and currency instruments.

References

Alexander, Ian, and Chia Shi-Chien. 2002. "Bond Finance: A Growing Source of Funds for Utility and Infrastructure Companies?" *International Journal of Regulation and Governance* 2 (1): 1–25.

Bakovic, Tonci, Bernard Tenenbaum, and Fiona Woolf. 2003. "Regulation by Contract, A New Way to Privatize Electricity Distribution." Working Paper 14, World Bank, Washington, DC.

Costain, Juan, and Mark Dutz. 2004. "Investment Promotion and Finance Facility." Concept Note, World Bank, Washington, DC.

Dailami, Mansoor. 2004. "The Challenge of Financing Infrastructure in Developing Countries." In World Bank, *Global Development Finance* 2004, 149–166. Washington, DC.

Euromoney. 2006. "Securitizations in Latin America." Seminar, Miami, May 15–16.

Fay, Marianne, and Tito Yepes. 2003. "Investing in Infrastructure: What Is Needed from 2000 to 2010?" Policy Research Working Paper 3102, World Bank, Washington, DC.

Fitch Ratings. 2005. *2005 Report on LAC Structured Finance.* Paris.

Gray, Philip, and Tim Irwin. 2003. "Exchange Rate Risk, Reviewing the Record for Private Infrastructure Contracts." In *Public Policy for the Private Sector,* note 262. Washington, DC: World Bank.

Guasch, J. Luis. 2004. *Granting and Renegotiating Infrastructure Concessions, Avoiding the Pitfalls.,* Washington, DC: World Bank.

Haarmeyer, David, and Ashoka Mody. 1998. "Financing Water and Sanitation Projects—the Unique Risks." Viewpoint Note 151, World Bank, Washington, DC.

Harris, Clive. 2003. "Private Participation in Infrastructure in Developing Countries." Working Paper 5, World Bank, Washington, DC.

Izaguirre, Ada Karina. 2004. "Private Infrastructure: Activity Down by 30 Percent in 2002." Public Policy for the Private Sector Note 267, World Bank, Washington, DC.

Kehew, Robert, Tomoko Matsukawa, and John Petersen. 2005. "Local Financing for Sub-Sovereign Infrastructure in Developing Countries: Case Studies of Innovative Domestic Credit Enhancement Entities and Techniques." Infrastructure, Economics, and Finance Department Discussion Paper 1, World Bank, Washington, DC.

Klingebiel, Daniela, and Jeff Ruster. 2000. "Why Infrastructure Facilities Often Fall Short of Their Objectives." Policy Research Working Paper 2358, World Bank, Washington, DC.

Leipziger, Danny. 2004. "The Status of Infrastructure Reform in Latin America." World Bank, Washington, DC.

Matsukawa, Tomoko, Robert Sheppard, and Joseph Wright. 2003. "Foreign Exchange Risk Mitigation for Power and Water Projects in Developing Countries." Energy and Mining Sector Board Discussion Paper 9, World Bank, Washington, DC.

Noel, Michel, and W. Jan Brzeski. 2004. "Mobilizing Private Finance for Local Infrastructure in Europe and Central Asia: An Alternative PPP Framework." Policy Research Working Paper, World Bank, Washington, DC.

Noel, Michel, and Sophie Sirtaine. Forthcoming. "Making Capital Markets Work for Infrastructure Finance." Working Paper, World Bank, Washington, DC.

Sirtaine, Sophie, and Luis De La Plaza. 2004. "New Approaches to Attract and Finance Private Sector Participation in Infrastructure." World Bank, Washington, DC.

Thobani, Matteen. 1998. "Private Infrastructure, Public Risk." *Economic Policy Notes* 10. World Bank, Washington, DC.

World Bank. 1996. *Infrastructure Development in East Asia and the Pacific: Toward a New Public-Private Partnership.* Washington, DC.

CHAPTER 4

Structured Finance for SMEs

SMEs are important in the economies of Latin America, but they frequently face difficulties in obtaining credit from the formal financial sector, including commercial banks and nonbank financial institutions. Their financing of working capital and investment relies heavily on funds provided by owners, trade credit from suppliers, and credit from informal lenders. This type of financing can be insufficient, constraining growth. The characteristics, maturities, and costs of informal credit are frequently inadequate for firms' financing needs.

Commercial bank lending to SMEs has been constrained by several factors. These include their comparatively high credit risk, lack of transparency, inadequate creditor protection by legal frameworks, high regulatory requirements in lending to them, and lack of innovation in financial products and credit risk methodologies tailored to SME characteristics.

Nonbank financial institutions such as factoring and leasing companies can be complementary sources of financing, but their impact is still moderate. Factoring companies provide short-term liquidity for working capital by purchasing otherwise idle accounts receivable. Leasing companies provide longer-term financing to cover SME investment needs for specific capital goods, such as machinery and equipment. Besides their direct impact on increasing financing, the leasing and factoring markets can enhance

competition and contestability in the financial sector. But leasing and factoring industries have had a relatively modest impact on Latin American
financial sectors, often due to the absence of an adequate legal framework.

Structured finance, particularly through asset securitizations, can
enhance financing to SMEs in the long run by creating a channel between
institutional investors and SME borrowers. Asset securitization can convert
pools of illiquid and relatively high-risk assets into low-risk tradable securities that can appeal to such institutional investors as pension funds. Over
the past two years, securitizations have gained momentum in Brazil and
Mexico after significant improvements in the legal and regulatory frameworks. The market for these instruments is nascent—but growing—in other
countries such as Argentina and Peru. And many of these transactions have
been made by subinvestment-grade[1] medium firms, which were previously
unable to tap securities markets. While these operations require sizable
volumes to appeal to institutional investors and justify the transaction costs
for originators, some transactions have successfully reached this minimum
by pooling receivables from midsize originators. But securitizations may
not suit small companies. For them, alternative mechanisms such as factoring, leasing, or warehouse financing may be more affordable.

Securitization can also help financial institutions increase their credit
to SMEs by providing an appealing source of financing for their SME
exposure. For small banks and such nonbank financial institutions as leasing and factoring firms, securitizations can be an efficient financing mechanism. Larger commercial banks may not require funding or liquidity
(they benefit from a wide deposit base). Securitization can transfer the
credit risk of their SME loan portfolio to the market and expand their loan
portfolio without requiring them to increase their capital.

But developing markets active in securitizing SME-related assets have several requirements. First, a robust primary market must exist with sizable volumes, a long track record, and fairly standardized assets. Second, the legal and
regulatory framework must allow this type of securitization. Third, the development of securitization markets can be costly, so active government participation is important. Fourth, securitizations can only complement overall
SME financing. They cannot substitute for credit from financial institutions,
and they are unsuitable for those firms needing equity rather than debt.

SMEs in Latin American Economies and Their Limited Access to Finance

SMEs have a significant role in Latin American economies (figure 4.1).

Figure 4.1. Number of SMEs by Country, 2002

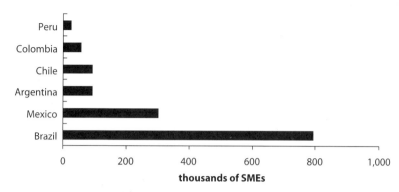

Source: Ramos (2003).

Note: SMEs are companies with fewer than 250 employees.

Steadily growing, this segment accounts for more than 25 percent of employment and 30 percent of production in many Latin American countries (IADB 2001). Some studies link the development in this market segment with overall economic growth (Beck and others 2004).

But funding from the formal financial sector has not fueled the growth in SMEs. The most important source of SME financing in Latin America comes from owners, through additional equity or reinvested profits. In recent World Bank surveys, these funds accounted for 40–60 percent of total financing for companies in many Latin American countries. Other studies have found that trade credits are the second most important source, much more important than bank credit (figure 4.2).

SME access to financial sector credit varies significantly across Latin America, not necessarily linked to a country's overall macroeconomic situation. More than 70 percent of SMEs recently surveyed in Chile obtain financing mainly from commercial banks (World Bank forthcoming). But fewer than 17 percent of medium companies in Mexico consider banks their main source of credit, and the proportion is even lower among smaller companies (Banco de México 2005). The high cost of credit, stringent application requirements, lack of qualifying collateral,[2] and the absence of financial products to meet SME characteristics are frequently cited as the main obstacles.[3] These conditions have often been justified by the higher defaults among SMEs than among larger firms. But bank perceptions of SME credit risk can also be unduly high (IADB 2001).

Figure 4.2. Sources of Financing for Companies in Latin America

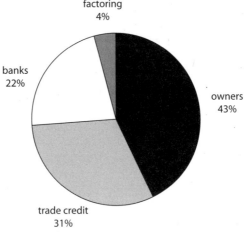

Source: Ramos (2003).

Factoring and leasing can be important sources of finance, complementing—rather than substituting for—the activities of commercial banks. By design, factoring and leasing firms better mitigate SME credit risks because their products are more closely aligned with the characteristics of these firms. Yet their full potential has yet to be tapped in Latin America. Many countries lack specific and comprehensive legal, regulatory, taxation, and accounting frameworks (annexes 4.1 and 4.2). Leasing and factoring companies can also improve the behavior of banks and other large financial institutions. When owned and managed independently, they can stimulate innovation and increase the contestability of financial markets, creating incentives for banks to become more responsive to the needs of their customers, expand the range of their financial services, and even lower their spreads.

Capital markets have provided limited funding to SMEs, despite important attempts to facilitate their access (box 4.1). The fixed costs of equity and debt issues do not make it economically viable for them to raise capital directly through capital markets. Their small issues do not justify the costs for institutional investors to analyze them individually. In addition, debt issued by SMEs would hardly achieve a credit rating that would appeal to institutional investors without credit enhancements (such as guarantees). And most SMEs are not ready for the discipline, formality, governance, and disclosure required by capital markets. Even private equity flows to Latin America are limited (about 10 percent of global

Box 4.1

Financing SMEs through the Stock Market

Several Latin American countries have attempted to create direct access to capital markets by SMEs as a way to enhance financing opportunities:

- Brazil created the Novo Mercado (or small-cap market).
- The Chilean stock exchange began targeting SMEs in 2001 by making it easier for them to be publicly traded.
- Colombia lowered the minimum threshold for listings to less than US$200,000 in assets.
- Mexico's 2005 securities law created a new legal form for enterprises that want to attract private equity, leading to a potential future listing. Its impact has yet to be measured.

But SME access to equity markets has not materialized. After a promising start, stocks of Chilean SMEs were seldom traded, and the limited exit opportunities led to losses and negative perceptions of the market. Listings in other markets have not yet gained momentum.

flows), due to inadequate minority shareholder rights and the low probability of successful exit through initial public offerings. Exit through sale to other companies remains viable.

Securitization to Enhance the Financing of SMEs

Securitizations can enhance financing to SMEs by creating a channel from institutional investors. Asset securitization has proved an efficient mechanism to convert illiquid and relatively high-risk SME-related assets into tradable securities that have the creditworthiness required by such institutional investors as pension funds.

There is a nascent market for securitizing SME-related assets in Latin America. As mentioned in previous chapters, activity in structured bond markets in Latin America has taken off in the past two years. While issuance has been dominated by bonds backed by mortgages and consumer credit, several transactions involved SME-related assets—that is, credit owed to or by SMEs. The universe of companies tapping the capital markets has expanded, including firms whose size and creditworthiness would have prevented them from issuing ordinary corporate debt (table 4.1).

Table 4.1. Securitizations of SME-Related Assets in Latin America, 2004–05

Country	Originator	Size of originator	Sector	Industry	Securitized assets	Amount (millions)	Rating
Argentina	Various agricultural producers	SME	Agriculture	Agriculture	Trade receivables	Arg$19.94	arAA+
Argentina	Various agricultural producers	SME	Agriculture	Agriculture	Trade receivables	US$1.5	arA+
Brazil	Ficap	Large	Manufacturing	Cable and wires	Trade receivables	R$40	arAA+
Brazil	Braskem	Large	Manufacturing	Petrochemicals	Trade receivables	R$400	arAA
Brazil	Gradiente	SME	Services	Retail trade	Trade receivables	R$78.8	arAA
Brazil	Petroflex	SME	Manufacturing	Rubber manufacturing	Trade receivables	R$60	brAAA
Brazil	Spinelli	SME	Nonbank financial institution (NBFI)	Brokerage	Trade receivables	R$10	brA
Brazil	Zoomp	SME	Manufacturing	Textiles	Trade receivables	R$48	brAAA
Mexico	Hipotecaria Su Casita	SME	NBFI	Mortgage and construction finance	Construction bridge loans	US$100	AAA
Mexico	Hipotecaria Su Casita	SME	NBFI	Mortgage and construction finance	Construction bridge loans	Mex$137	mxA
Mexico	Infu Trust	SME	Services	Leasing of commercial real estate	Income rights—concession	US$180	BBB
Mexico	Infu Trust	SME	Services	Leasing of commercial real estate	Income rights—concession	UDIs$190	BBB
Mexico	Vitro	Large	Manufacturing	Glass	Trade receivables	Mex$550	mxAAA
Mexico	Corporación Metropolitana de Arrendamientos	Medium	Services	Leasing of machinery and equipment	Partial guarantee	Mex$80	mxA
Mexico	Corporación GEO	Large	Construction	Construction	Trade receivables	Mex$453	mxAAA
Mexico	Servicios Financieros Navistar	Medium	NBFI (captive financial)	Transport equipment	Loans to SMEs	Mex$516	mxAAA
Peru	Drokasa	SME	Manufacturing	Pharmaceutical	Trade receivables	US$25	AAA[a]
Peru	Cineplex	SME	Services	Leisure	Trade receivables	US$8	—
Peru	Continental Bolsa	SME	NBFI		Trade receivables	US$50	—

Source: Standard & Poor's Emerging Markets Ratings List, Moody's 2005 Review Latin American ABS/MBS, and Equilibrium Clasificadora de Riesgo (Peru).

Note: This list was compiled from rating agencies and so may not be exhaustive. UDIs = Unidades de Inversion.

a. Local scale rating assigned by local rating agency.

Securitizations of accounts receivable have become commonplace in various countries. In 2004–05, there were more than 10 issues of structured bonds backed by accounts receivable in Brazil, and similar transactions have begun in Mexico, Peru, and Argentina. So far, other SME-related assets, such as loans and leasing contracts, have not been securitized in the region, though practitioners expect this soon. Securitizations have proved a versatile financing instrument for different types of assets, originators, and amounts. The amounts issued through securitizations ranged from US$4 million to more than US$200 million (table 4.1). The originators ranged from petrochemical and construction material firms to clothing and retail firms. And many are medium in size. Practitioners expect that even smaller originators will be able to tap the market by pooling their assets in joint securitizations, as in recent transactions in Argentina and Peru (box 4.2).

The common denominator in these transactions is that the structured bonds achieved the highest ratings in their local markets, well above those of the originators. Vitro, a Mexican manufacturer of construction materials, has a noninvestment-grade credit rating of mxBB+, which would make its debt issues ineligible for investment by pension funds. But the structured bonds backed by Vitro's trade receivables reached a credit rating equal to that of government debt (mxAAA).

Securitizations can only be a complement to other financing mechanisms and have yet to develop. Securitizations cannot replace the need for financing through bank credit lines, ordinary bond issuance, and equity. But they can be a significant alternative source of financing for companies able to use them. Securitizations can, however, be costly to structure and issue, and they impose high requirements on issuers. Until now, the number and volume of SME-related securitizations in the region has been relatively modest compared with mortgage-backed securities (chapter 2).

Development of primary credit markets for SMEs has been lackluster in most of Latin America, limiting the pool of securitizable assets. Securitizations require a vast pool of cash flow–generating assets to achieve a fairly diversified portfolio, reach minimal issuance size to cover structuring costs, and avoid deterioration of the originator's creditworthiness.[4] But the limited credit from financial institutions to SMEs in Latin America has constrained the size of lenders' credit portfolios,[5] limiting their access to financial markets through securitizations. One way to overcome the limited securitizable pool is to pool several originators, which itself poses challenges (box 4.2).

In revolving securitizations—the main structure observed so far for SMEs—the ability of the originator to keep generating good assets must

> **Box 4.2**
>
> ## Multi-Originator Securitizations
>
> Pooling portfolios from various originators into one securitization can create a large volume of assets and achieve diversification. These transactions can help originators reach the critical mass required by the market and benefit from economies of scale. Multi-originator transactions have been arranged in Colombia and Argentina through specialized conduits.
>
> But these transactions have been based on more standardized assets, such as mortgage loans. Going forward, one of the main requirements for multi-originator transactions with SME-related assets will be homogenizing the basic characteristics of these assets—as well as their origination and administration processes. This requirement, and the fact that originators are jointly affected by losses in the overall portfolio, can make multi-originator transactions more viable for companies that belong to the same industrial group or trade association.
>
> Investment funds are an attractive alternative to multi-originator bonds. Created in 2004 in Peru, a pilot SME receivables investment fund is being studied for replication. The Brazilian FIDCs also have features that allow them to function as multi-originator conduits.

be proven. Where the maturity of securitized assets is significantly shorter than that of the securitization, transactions are usually revolving—that is, a matured receivable is substituted by one of similar quality and characteristics.[6] Revolving transactions have an additional operational risk, the ability of the originator to continue originating assets with characteristics similar to those of the original securitized pool. This risk, usually assessed by analyzing the track record of the originator, is mitigated through covenants that trigger the termination of the transaction if ability of the originator to supply the qualifying assets is compromised or if the securitized portfolio deteriorates.

Originators must have clear and consistent credit and collection procedures, as well as representative and reliable historical information on the performance of SME assets. Securitizations work best when the underlying assets are homogeneous and have similar credit risk profiles and cash flow characteristics. Credit to SMEs, either from financial institutions or from commercial creditors, is usually more difficult to standardize than, say, mortgages. Commercial loans are usually tailored to companies' needs in maturity, amortization, currency, and collateral. Similarly, the conditions of trade credit usually vary significantly depending on the companies providing and receiving it. Standardized credit origination and collection procedures can ensure some homogeneity of the current and future assets in the securitized portfolio. In addition, analyzing the creditworthiness of most SME securitizations requires calculating future cash flows expected from the pool of assets. This calculation is based on the historical performance of the portfolio of the originator and relies on its historical information on default rates,[7] timing, and proportion of recoveries on nonperforming assets.[8] Long and comprehensive datasets from the originator will enhance transaction viability.

Inadequate securities instruments or limited regulatory resources may constrain the development of the market. The introduction of securities instruments that balance flexibility and cost efficiency for issuers against security for investors (FIDCs in Brazil and CBs in Mexico) has been a major factor in the development of the most active securitization markets in Latin America. At the same time, the diversity and relative complexity of these instruments require that securities authorities develop capabilities that avoid unnecessary hurdles and transaction costs in approving and monitoring them.

Securitizing Accounts Receivable

Accounts receivable freeze a sizable share of company assets. In the course of operations, companies usually provide short-term financing to their clients in the sale of products or services. This trade credit is usually granted for 30–90 days, with an implicit financing cost for the client.[9] For companies providing credit to their clients, the accounts receivable are idle assets that take resources out of their main commercial or productive activities and enhance their need for financing.

Securitizations help Latin American companies obtain liquidity through the sale of accounts receivable. Transactions based on accounts receivable (also called trade receivables) dominate the market for securitizations of SME assets in Latin America. The most active market for this type of securities is in Brazil, with a volume of more than US$535 million in 2004 (box 4.3).

The potential benefits of securitizations for originators:

- Freeing resources from trade receivables, which can be used to finance operations, repay existing debts, or support new productive investments.
- Reaching higher levels of creditworthiness, bringing down overall financing costs below those of traditional bank credit lines.

- Diversifying funding sources toward less reliance on banks.
- Improving asset and liability management by matching expected cash flows with debt repayments.
- Accessing the securities markets for new originators (box 4.3).

Box 4.3

Securitization of Trade Receivables in Brazil—FIDC Zoomp

Zoomp S.A., a Brazilian clothing label, entered the local securities markets for the first time in 2005 through a R$48 million (roughly US$23 million) three-year securitization program of trade receivables, using the popular FIDC structure. The transaction achieved a rating of brAAAf, the highest in the Brazilian local market, which translated into a yield only nine basis points above the interbank reference rate.

The Structure and Participants
The assets backing the transaction are trade credit receivables generated through the sale of the originators' products to multibrand retailers and franchised shops. The mechanism of the transaction (box figure):

- The transaction starts with the discounted sale of existing receivables from Zoomp to an FIDC, which operates as a bankruptcy-remote, special-purpose vehicle, managed by a professional independent asset manager. The discount on the face value of the receivables is intended to be the main source of interest payments for investors.
- The FIDC issues senior shares sold to institutional investors and subordinated shares kept by the originator. A large part of the proceeds from senior shares is used to pay to the originator (Zoomp) for the receivables sold. Part is maintained by the FIDC to create a liquidity reserve to repay investors.
- At maturity, trade receivables are paid to a custodian—in this case, a highly rated commercial bank. The custodian is in charge of transferring the funds to the FIDC. This eliminates the risk that payments of securitized receivables made directly to Zoomp could be diverted to other uses.
- One part of the funds collected through the custodian is allocated to the reserve account, the source of payment of interest and principal to investors. Another part is used to acquire additional receivables from Zoomp as a substitute for those matured.
- At the end of the transaction, the reserve account is used to pay to investors the final installment and the remainder, after payment of operating expenses for participants, is paid to Zoomp as the holder of the subordinated notes.

Box 4.3 (*continued*)

The Structure of the FIDC Zoomp

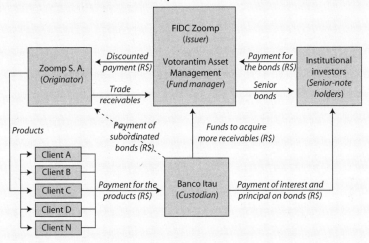

Mitigating the Risks

The creditworthiness of the fund shares sold to institutional investors is achieved through subordination. In this transaction, the main risk is default by Zoomp's clients. The assessment of this risk is determined through analyzing the historical performance of Zoomp's trade credit portfolio. Once assessed, this risk is covered by issuing two types of notes: senior notes offered to institutional investors and subordinated notes kept by the originator (20 percent of the total issuance). Because senior-note holders have the first claim on the fund's assets, the securitized portfolio has to suffer losses beyond 20 percent of its value before senior-note holders are affected. Holding subordinated notes, Zoomp receives payments only after full repayment of principal and interest to senior-note holders. Zoomp assumes any losses below 20 percent, creating incentives to generate creditworthy trade receivables.

The possible deterioration of portfolio credit quality also poses a risk to investors. Given its revolving nature and the short term of the portfolio securitized, the transaction relies heavily on Zoomp's ability to originate receivables of similar credit quality and characteristics to those originally securitized. It is thus essential that the originator can demonstrate a good track record in originating trade receivables. Strict eligibility criteria ensure that matured assets in the transaction portfolio are substituted by other assets of similar characteristics and quality. In this case, the custodian is in charge of constantly monitoring the quality of the portfolio.

Source: Standard & Poor's (2005).

The Link between Factoring and SME Securitization

Small firms may not be able to access financing through securitizations due to scale requirements. The significant fixed costs in securitization transactions—and the volumes required to appeal to institutional investors—rule out most small companies from accessing this market. And pooling assets into a combined portfolio may not be viable for small firms, because the process is complex and poses significant operating costs. For small firms, discounting trade receivables with a formal factoring company may provide most of the benefits of securitization while avoiding high additional operating costs.

Factoring firms can, in turn, securitize their receivables portfolios to reach higher creditworthiness on their bonds issuance. Factoring firms are SMEs themselves in many countries, especially when they are not part of a financial group. Their main sources of financing are bank credit lines and—for the most creditworthy—issuance of bonds in the capital markets. Securitizations could facilitate their access to the securities market. There have not been any securitizations by factoring firms in Latin America, but practitioners consider this likely soon. The Brazilian factoring association has been working on setting up a small multi-originator FIDC, backed by the sale of receivables from several factoring firms.

Securitizing SME Leasing Contracts

Securitizations of leasing contracts use a similar framework to those of trade receivables. Instruments such as the Brazilian FIDCs or Mexican CBs provide enough flexibility to cater to different types of originators and assets. The main differences between securitizations of trade receivables and those of leasing contracts are the originators and the assets (table 4.2). All other aspects are the same and so are not addressed here.

Table 4.2. Differences between Securitizations of Trade Receivables and Leasing Contracts

Originator	Asset securitized	Maturity of the assets securitized
Commercial, services, or manufacturing firm	Existing and future trade receivables from the sale of products or services	Short, usually 30–90 days
Leasing companies (including financial institutions in many countries)	Future flows from contracts for leasing of capital goods (machinery, automobiles, computers)	Medium, usually more than a year

The main benefit of securitizations for leasing companies is the greater potential to access funding through capital markets. Unlike banks, leasing companies do not benefit from low-cost funding through deposits. Their funding sources are mostly expensive bank credit lines—and in some cases, financing from parent companies.[10] Only the largest and most creditworthy leasing firms have been able to tap the capital markets directly. For leasing firms with lower credit ratings, securitizing their existing leasing portfolios can generate significant benefits:

- Expanding their operations using an additional funding source.
- Accessing capital markets with high-credit-quality instruments, even when the credit rating of the firm is below that required by institutional investors.
- Diversifying funding sources toward less reliance on banks.
- Reducing the cost of financing to a level that can be well below that of bank credit lines.
- Improving asset-liability management through matching maturities.
- Improving liquidity.

The relative homogeneity of leasing contracts makes them particularly suitable for securitization. Leasing contracts usually have similar maturities, are relatively standardized, and have homogeneous cash flows and similar types of collateral. The relatively long maturities of leasing contracts matches the (usually) long terms of securitization transactions.

Prospects for Leasing Securitizations in Latin America

Relatively new, securitizations of leasing contracts are still smaller than other types of asset-backed securities. Sperry Lease Finance, a North American leasing firm, executed the first leasing securitization in 1985, and these transactions have become fairly widespread in some developed capital markets. In 2003, the annual volume of securitizations of equipment lease contracts in the United States was about US$70 billion, equivalent to a third of the country's annual leasing volume. The proportion is similar in some European countries (Italy, for example). Securitizations of leasing contracts in emerging markets have been infrequent, more often one-off transactions than part of wider programs.

The prerequisite for the development of leasing securitization is a well-developed primary leasing market. The volume of the leasing sector's operations in Latin America is still modest. As a result, the potential for leasing securitizations may be limited until leasing is adequately developed as an SME funding tool. Some leasing companies have started to tap the securities markets through structured debt issuances, though these are still not backed by leasing contracts.[11] According to practitioners, full-scale securitizations of leasing assets are in the pipeline.

Multi-originator leasing securitization could help reach the critical mass to tap into capital markets, but it poses additional challenges. In countries where the leasing sector is small or leasing companies are non-diversified niche players, pooling contracts from various leasing companies may create the critical mass and diversification. But this requires their willingness to operate jointly in the structure and poses the additional problem of standardizing origination and servicing procedures across the participants. There are no legal constraints on the minimum size of a securitization transaction, but a fairly large amount must be issued to make the transaction costs viable. Leasing securitization transactions in developing markets have been above US$50 million, but other Latin American domestic securitizations suggest that transactions could be as small as US$20 million and still attract institutional investors and justify costs.

Securitizing Commercial Loans to SMEs

Even though securitization of loans is common in other regions, this market has been inactive in Latin America. Securitizations of loans, known as collateralized loan obligations, are fairly common in many developed financial markets. They apply to SME loans when commercial banks have significant penetration in the SME segment, as in the United States, Spain, Italy, and Germany. In most Latin American countries, commercial bank portfolios of SME loans are slim due to lackluster bank credit activity in this segment in the past few years.

Existing transactions in Latin America have been originated by non-bank financial institutions. The credit activities of nonbank financial institutions (finance companies, savings banks, credit unions, and—to lesser extent—microfinance institutions [MFIs])[12] in the SME market in Latin America have grown significantly, if from a small base. Structured transactions in the region have been originated by nonbank financial institutions. One recent example is the securitization of loans to acquire machinery by Servicios Financieros Navistar in Mexico (box 4.4). A second transaction is the 2005 securitization of bridge loans to construction companies originated by Hipotecaria Su Casita, a housing finance company in Mexico. The transaction had a cross-border component (with US$100 million rated AAA based on a guarantee from Financial Security Assurance)[13] and a local component (with Mex$137 million rated mxA). And in Peru, the

Box 4.4

Securitization of Loans to SMEs in Mexico

In December 2004, Servicios Financieros Navistar (SFN), a nonbank captive financial institution,[a] securitized a portfolio of 1,545 loans (most of them to SMEs) for
the local currency equivalent of about US$50 million. This transaction achieved
the highest rating in the local market (mxAAA) and was subscribed at a variable
interest rate of 128 basis points above the interbank rate (8.75 percent at the date
of issuance).

All loans in the transaction were provided by SFN in sales of Navistar equipment to clients. These loans have an average original maturity of 40 months and
carry a fixed interest averaging 17.83 percent—providing a comfortable differen-
tial of 1,000 basis points compared with the yield to investors at issuance. This
transaction was static—that is, all loans transferred to the market existed at the
beginning of the transaction and they would not be substituted by new assets
once they mature.

Mitigating Risks

The creditworthiness of the bonds issued was based on several credit-enhancement
mechanisms:

1. Issuance of subordinated notes that are kept by SFN and that receive payment
   only after full repayment of the interest and principal to senior-note holders.
2. A liquidity reserve constituted with a portion (10 percent) of the proceeds of
   the sale of senior notes to investors.
3. A partial guarantee covering part (17 percent) of the principal of the senior
   notes provided by Nacional Financiera (Nafin), a government-owned development bank.[b]
4. An interest rate hedging instrument contracted to cover differentials
   between the variable interest rate paid to senior-note holders and the fixed
   interest rate paid by SFN's borrowers.

The bonds issued were CBs, and the mechanism is as follows (see box figure).

- SFN transferred existing loans with a combined outstanding balance of
  Mex$539 million to an issuing trust (a special-purpose vehicle) managed by
  an investment bank.
- The special-purpose vehicle issued a set of senior notes for Mex$516 million,
  which were sold to investors and had a maturity of 36 months, with monthly

(Box continues on the following page.)

Box 4.4 (*continued*)

repayment of interest and principal (this shows the flexibility of this bond instrument).
- SFN received Mex$464 million from the proceeds of bonds sold to investors. The remnant was maintained by the special-purpose vehicle as a liquidity reserve.
- Subordinated notes for Mex$26 million (4.5 percent of the portfolio) were maintained by SFN.
- Payments from SFN clients are collected in an account set up by the special-purpose vehicle manager.[c]
- The partial guarantee from Nafin is exercised only if losses in the portfolio affect senior-note holders.

The Mechanism of the SFN Transaction

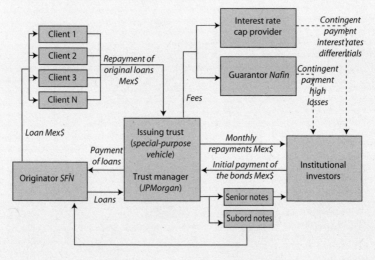

Source: Standard & Poor's (2004).

a. SFN is a subsidiary of Navistar International Corp., a North American manufacturer of truck and buses. Although SFN is a financial institution, it provides financing only to dealerships and clients of Navistar for the purchase of Navistar's transport equipment, hence its status as captive financial firm.

b. Note that the figures corresponding to the level of subordination, the proportion of the liquidity reserve, and the guarantee provided by Nafin, are derived from the analysis of the cash flow of the transaction and are presented here for illustration purposes, but they are not representative of other operations.

c. In case of bankruptcy of the originator, a servicing company is hired to continue monitoring and servicing payments from the loans. This servicing company is usually identified and a contingent contract is signed as part of the structuring of the transaction.

World Bank provided technical assistance to the securities regulator (Comisión Nacional Supervisora de Empresas y Valores) to facilitate the development of multi-originator securitizations of micro and small loans provided by savings banks (cajas municipales de ahorro y crédito). A pilot transaction was expected to reach the market in 2006.

Benefits of SME Loan Portfolio Securitization for Originators

For smaller or less creditworthy commercial banks and nonbank financial institutions, the main benefits are enhancing financing opportunities, as for leasing and factoring firms. Securitizations can help smaller (and frequently less creditworthy) financial intermediaries to obtain funding, reduce financing costs, and diversify funding sources through access to securities markets. These transactions can also provide other benefits, such as better asset-liability management through matching maturities, diversified sources of income,[14] capital relief (see below), and initial contact with the market, which could lead to easier market access and less credit enhancement in further issuances.

For larger or highly creditworthy commercial banks, the most important benefit is capital relief. Large commercial banks can obtain cheap financing through usually ample deposit bases and usually have high creditworthiness in local financial markets. That enables them to issue ordinary bonds or long-term deposit products, with relatively low yields. Accordingly, the transaction costs of securitizations, credit enhancements, and fees to participants can make these transactions more expensive than traditional sources of funding available to larger financial intermediaries. For these intermediaries, securitizations can be more appealing as a capital relief mechanism.[15]

Through securitizations, banks can transfer to the market the credit risk of their SME loans, freeing up the capital set aside for them. This capital relief can enhance the capacity of lenders to maintain or even increase the origination of SME credit without requiring additional capital, enhancing their incentives for SME lending. In many cases, active securitization markets have helped banks become more agile intermediaries between institutional investors and borrowers, introducing a significant fee-based revenue component.[16]

However, not all securitizations provide capital relief. A common feature in the transactions reviewed here is that originators provided a credit enhancement by maintaining a subordinated participation. In those cases, the expected flows are transferred to investors but the originator maintains most of the credit risk of the underlying assets. Capital relief is achieved only when the originator does not hold a subordinated participation or when its subordinated participation is smaller (as a proportion of the securitized pool) than the regulatory capital requirements for the whole securitized pool. In other regions, some transactions are designed to transfer only the credit risk to the market, while the originator maintains the property of the underlying assets. These credit derivatives are not allowed in some Latin American countries, apparently due to concerns about investors' ability to assess and correctly price the risk taken.

Government Support for SME Loan Securitizations

Support provided by governments, public entities, or multilateral organizations has been instrumental in the development of SME securitizations in various countries. Indeed, the development of securitization markets—conducting extensive legal due diligence, setting up instruments, and educating market participants and potential investors—can be costly. These costs are usually covered by the first issuers, but once the market is developed, new issuers can benefit substantially by issuing securities with similar characteristics. The primary development of the market is thus akin to a public good that private issuers may not be willing to cover. In this context, the active participation of governments in enabling the development of these markets is important. Such support has been provided through credit-enhancement facilities (such as partial guarantees at borrower level), partial credit guarantees for the securitization of loan portfolios, or market infrastructure and intermediation.

Government Support at the Borrower Level

Governments can support SME financing through the provision of direct guarantees on loans to SMEs, but this requires adequate guarantee design and pricing to align incentives and minimize fiscal cost. The main rationale for these guarantees is that lenders may not lend to SMEs, given their perceived high credit risk, lack of credit history, and lenders' lack of systematic screening and risk assessment processes. By sharing the credit risk with lenders through partial guarantees, governments aim at enhancing lender incentives to start or increase lending. In turn, banks are expected to develop knowledge of the market and tailored credit risk management processes that enable them to maintain SME lending even after the guarantee is eventually phased out. Experience in Latin America has yielded mixed results,[17] but generally it seems important that lenders remain exposed to some credit risk to have an incentive to originate and manage guaranteed loans efficiently. A more detailed analysis of Latin American guarantee programs is needed, but so far there is little evidence of successful phase-outs of such guarantees or thorough impact analysis of additional lending to SMEs.

In the United States, a Small Business Administration (SBA) program provides a partial guarantee on SME loans granted by participating financial institutions, both banks and finance companies. The guarantee covers all loans that comply with a set of requirements defined by the SBA, both in the characteristics of the borrower and the structuring of the loan.[18] The lender maintains the responsibility for originating the loans and evaluating the creditworthiness of borrowers. The guarantee is partial, covering up to 80 percent of the loan granted. But the cost of the guarantee for lenders is linked to the amount covered, which in a competitive market can provide a balance between the risk that the lender is willing to take and the price that it is willing to pay.[19] Sharing the risk of borrower default reduces moral hazard and creates incentives to ensure good credit screening and monitoring.

In a securitization, the SBA partially guaranteed loans can be bundled and transferred to the market, as has been done since 1985. Through this mechanism, more than US$25 billion in loans guaranteed by the SBA from various participating lenders have been securitized through pooled portfolios. In this program, government support enabled the primary origination of the SME loans, which thereafter were transferred to the market. In subsequent programs, government support was more focused on facilitating the securitization of loans already originated by lenders.

Government Support at the Portfolio Level: Partial Guarantees on Securitization[20]

In Spain, a government program aims to support lending to SMEs by fostering the securitization of these loans. In 1999, the Spanish government created the Fondo de Titulización de Activos Pyme (FTPYME) program to enhance SME financing through supporting the securitization of existing SME loans from commercial lenders. The objective is to help lenders unload part of their portfolio into the market and obtain liquidity and capital relief that could be used to originate further SME loans. The government initially provided a partial credit guarantee to reduce the financial costs of the transactions and add comfort for institutional investors, which were not initially accustomed to these transactions.

The FTPYME program granted a direct and irrevocable partial guarantee from the Spanish Treasury to qualifying transactions. At present, the guarantee covers up to 80 percent of AA-rated tranches within a given transaction,[21] about 20 percent of the total issuance in recent transactions. As the market developed, the government guarantee has been gradually phased out, thus reducing the fiscal burden.[22] To ensure that this program enhances access to financing by smaller companies, the government required that at least 80 percent of the securitized portfolio be loans to SMEs.[23] And banks originating these assets are also required to use at least 80 percent of the proceeds of the transaction to provide additional financing to SMEs. These eligibility criteria are based on the fact that the cost of the guarantee provided by the government is lower than that of a privately contracted credit guarantee, so it is important not to use the implicit subsidy to finance large corporate companies.

The program has benefited financial institutions of all sizes, from the large first-tier commercial banks to smaller regional savings and loans institutions. For smaller institutions, the initial barrier posed by the relatively high critical mass required for a transaction has been eliminated through the pooling of assets in multi-originator transactions. The program is flexible enough to incorporate different types of assets, including loans, leasing receivables, and commercial mortgages.

The program supported the development of a previously marginal market for SME securitization in Spain. The market grew from €1.6 billion in 2000 to €8.8 billion in 2004. FTPYME securities have been widely accepted by both local and international institutional investors such as pensions and mutual funds.

The rapid development of the SME securitization market in Spain was underpinned by an existing framework for collateralized loan obligations. The type of securities required for SME loans securitizations (collateralized loan obligations) had been used in the Spanish market before the FTPYME program. Even though the underlying assets in previous Spanish collateralized loan obligations had been mainly the debt of larger corporations, the regulatory framework and the mechanisms for investor and borrower protection in these transactions are identical, so institutional investors were already familiar with these instruments. In many Latin American markets, the development of securitization markets for SME assets may take longer, given the lack of substantial precedent.

Government Support through Developing SME Securitization Infrastructure

In Germany, a government program reduces transaction costs for securitizations. The Programme for Mittelstand-loan Securitization (PROMISE), managed by Kreditantstalt für Wiederaufbau (KfW) in Germany, aims at enhancing SME financing by providing the means for lenders to transfer the credit risk of existing SME loans to the market. The capital relief through these transactions is expected to allow German banks to expand their loan origination without additional capital. The underlying benefit of the program is that it drastically reduces the transaction costs in securitizations through the use of an existing platform and a tested legal structure that investors, intermediaries, and regulators are familiar with. This program is based on synthetic transactions,[24] because KfW was seeking explicitly a mechanism to help lenders only with capital relief. A similar program for true sale transactions would provide the same main benefits in reducing transaction costs to originators.

In PROMISE transactions, KfW acts only as an intermediary, to help originating banks transfer to the market the unexpected losses of the reference portfolio. Banks pay a premium and retain the expected losses (the first loss position, typically about 3 percent). Since originators maintain the property of the underlying loans, the size of the pool is well above that of the actual bonds issued. KfW takes the credit risk of the reference pool from the originating bank (after first loss) and transfers it to financial institutions (through credit default swaps) and institutional investors (through credit-linked notes). Note that KfW does not retain any credit risk or provide any guarantees on the transactions.

The results of the program have been positive so far, with close to €15 billion issued. From 2000 to 2004, 11 transactions were issued under the PROMISE program, ranging from €200 million to €3.7 billion. Pension and investment funds have demonstrated considerable interest in these securities.

The benefits of the program are manifold for market participants. For lenders, besides the benefits of capital relief, through this mechanism, KfW provides equal access to capital markets to banks of different sizes. The common infrastructure of the program reduces significantly the transaction costs and facilitates the execution of transactions. In terms of deepening financial markets, the PROMISE program has helped to develop a secondary market for SME credit risk, with the associated price discovery benefit. For investors, PROMISE notes were a new asset class of high credit quality. For SMEs, the program is expected to translate into enhanced access to bank credit, though this impact has been difficult to quantify.

The Way Forward

The development of mechanisms that create a channel between institutional investors and SME borrowers requires active involvement of originators, authorities, and investors.

Originators

A strong primary market (for securitizable assets) is essential for the development of these financing mechanisms. Securitizations help originators expand their operations by providing liquidity through the transfer of existing assets to the market.

The strength of primary markets depends largely on the development of adequate products and processes by lenders. These products must recognize the underlying characteristics of borrowers and be based on clear and consistent origination processes. While standardization of terms and conditions of credit to SMEs—especially bank loans—may be difficult, lenders must strive to standardize processes and underwriting practices. To the extent that originators can demonstrate a consistent track record in origination, monitoring, and collection of their credits, access to markets will be facilitated.

Authorities

Authorities can facilitate the development of primary markets by ensuring the basic legal framework for credit operations. This is especially so for such instruments as factoring and leasing, which do not enjoy specific laws and regulations in various countries, reducing lender rights and increasing the cost of working out nonperforming accounts.

The development of adequate securities instruments facilitates market development, as in Brazil and Mexico. These instruments by themselves will not necessarily ignite a market in the absence of adequate macroeconomic and primary market conditions. But inadequate securitization vehicles and securities instruments can hinder the development of the market even when all other necessary conditions are present. The basic legal requirements for these instruments include the recognition of the concept of true sale of credit assets or the transfer of credit rights and the existence of regulations for a concept of special-purpose vehicles and the recognition of its bankruptcy remoteness.

Clear accounting and tax rules regarding securitizations must exist. If a securitization structure does keep some recourse to the originator (to replace deteriorating assets of the special-purpose vehicle), clarification is needed on whether the securitized assets should be kept on the balance sheet of the originator. Other rules that need to be sufficiently transparent include tax rules for originators regarding capital gains on assets transferred to the market.

Regulatory institutional capacity is paramount for the functioning of the market. The dynamic pace of securitization markets, along with the relative complexity of the transactions, poses challenges for authorities to acquire the skills and resources to maintain security in the system without unduly hindering or delaying approval of viable transactions. In addition, it would be useful to rethink the role of capital market supervisors when the main investors and instruments are "qualified"—that is, institutional investors—to strive for more agile issuance approvals.

In addition, the government can have an active role in the development of the market. Well-designed and -priced partial credit guarantees by the government can enhance SME lending activity, so a comprehensive analysis of successful partial credit guarantee schemes would be useful. The incentives offered to the market can be through partial guarantees at the level of borrower or the overall credit portfolio. Other government supports through securitization infrastructure (as in Germany) can help with the setup and transaction costs for participants without a significant ongoing fiscal cost for the government.

Investors
Institutional investors should be allowed to invest in new types of securities as long as their creditworthiness is within the limits of their investment rules. Securitizations can give investors a new asset class that provides appealing yields with high levels of creditworthiness. Within fund managers' mandate, institutional investors should develop the expertise to assess the risk and adequately price these instruments. Regulation should not impede investment in structured securities, especially when they possess a credit rating from an independent and recognized rating agency. Price vendors may be needed to help with marking to market when bonds are illiquid or nonstandard.

Annex 4.1. Factoring in Latin America

Invoice factoring, or purchase of receivables, presents several benefits to SMEs. Factoring improves the liquidity of a company by substituting accounts receivables with cash. It reduces the need for bank and supplier financing. Factors can often help recent startups and undercapitalized companies, since their main focus is the creditworthiness of the end-customers. Factoring companies tend to have fast and convenient service compared with that of banks. On the downside, factoring is typically a source of short-term working capital financing, not useful for capital expenditure.

The factoring process involves checking the quality of receivables, providing a cash advance, and keeping a reserve amount until the complete recovery of receivables. The factoring firm will conduct a lien search to determine if any lender has taken a first lien position in the business's accounts receivable as collateral. The factoring company focuses primarily on assessing the creditworthiness of the business customers, rather than that of the business itself. Invoices are eligible for factoring only once the services (or products) have been provided and accepted by the customer. Typically, an advance is made of 75–95 percent of the invoice value, and the difference, called the reserve, is held back until the customers pay the invoices in full. A fee and an agreed upon interest rate is deducted from the reserve. In emerging markets with ineffective movable collateral registries and credit bureaus, this factoring process may be more costly. A more promising variant is reverse factoring, which helps mitigate these issues in the specific case that the buyers of goods or services are more creditworthy (see box A4.1).

Another promising avenue in emerging markets is international factoring for export-oriented SMEs. This can be supported by the presence of international factoring company networks.[25] Annex box 4.2 provides an overview of how international factoring operations work. Based on available data, Chile is the only Latin American country with some international factoring activity, at only 5 percent of total factoring. In 2004, there were almost 5,500 Chilean companies with annual exports of less than US$1 million; this represents more than 80 percent of the total number of exporting companies, but only 2 percent of total country exports in volumes. Exporting SMEs would greatly benefit from the opportunity to offer credit terms on their sales to international clients. Factoring companies should often be able to offer such terms using their affiliation to the international factoring network. Similarly, in Brazil, exports rely heavily on foreign currency bank credit lines, making exporters vulnerable to external economic shocks. International factoring could reduce the need

Box A4.1

Reverse Factoring

In countries with weak credit information infrastructure, the case for several emerging market economies, factoring companies use a variant called "reverse factoring." In ordinary factoring, the factor (lender) generally purchases many accounts receivable from a limited number of sellers, which requires the factor to collect credit information and calculate the credit risk for a large number of customers. In reverse factoring, the factor purchases receivables payable by only a few high-quality customers from many smaller suppliers. Thus the lender needs to collect credit information and calculate the credit risk for only a few large, transparent, internationally accredited firms. Reverse factoring facilitates access to affordable finance to SMEs in emerging markets that supply goods and services to highly creditworthy, local, private companies and government and sub-sovereign entities. As such, this mechanism does not substitute for an existing factoring industry in a country, but it can complement it.

To make reverse factoring work, it is necessary to find incentives for large buyers to make it easier for their small providers to use factoring. This was identified as an issue in Chile, Peru, and Guatemala, because large clients typically like to use their negotiation advantage and keep the flexibility to request an extension from their small suppliers, while factored receivables have to be paid on time or a default is triggered. Part of the solution may be to emphasize the benefit to large clients through more favorable supplier credit terms.

A well-known example of reverse factoring is that implemented by Nafin, a Mexican development bank. A major feature of Nafin's program is the development of a Web-based system where participating large buyers report information on their accounts payable. This system is a trustable registry of active invoices, eliminating the risk of fraud. In this system, the supplier can discount the invoice through several different financial institutions (including banks and factors) participating in the program, which compete on price.

Because the source of the future payment of the invoice is a high-quality buyer, the credit risk assumed by financial institutions is low, which drives down the interest rates charged on these operations. The collection of receivables is also centralized in the system under Nafin's management, thereby reducing the administrative costs to both suppliers and buyers.

Source: Klapper (2004).

Box A4.2

International Factoring

When export factoring is carried out by members of an international factoring network, the service involves the following steps:

- The exporter signs a factoring contract assigning all agreed receivables to an export factor. The factor then becomes responsible for all aspects of the factoring operation.
- The export factor chooses a correspondent factoring firm to serve as an import factor in the country where the goods are to be shipped. The receivables are then reassigned to the import factor.
- In the meantime, the import factor investigates the credit standing of the buyer of the exported goods and establishes lines of credit, which allow the buyer to place an order on open account terms without opening letters of credit.
- Once the goods have been shipped, the export factor may advance up to 80 percent of the invoice value to the exporter.
- The import factor collects the full invoice value at maturity and is responsible for the swift transmission of funds to the export factor, which then pays the exporter the outstanding balance.
- If after 90 days past due date an approved invoice remains unpaid, the import factor will pay 100 percent of the invoice value under guarantee.

The process is designed to ensure risk-free export sales and allows exporting SMEs to offer more attractive terms to overseas customers without undue liquidity constraints or credit risks on new international clients.

Source: Factors Chain International.

for credit lines. In both Brazil and Chile, factoring firms are working to identify the obstacles to greater development of international factoring.

In Latin America, the use of factoring is generally limited—except for where it started in the 1980s and grew slowly—yet it currently services a significant number of SMEs. Factoring turnover in Latin America is still limited, except for Brazil, Mexico, and Chile (figure A4.1). This may be due to data issues. For example, some factoring activity exists in Nicaragua and Guatemala, but it is an unregulated activity and thus no data are collected. As of 2005, the factoring industry in Brazil, called *fomento mercantil*, contributes to financing the working capital needs of an estimated

100,000 SMEs that employ 2 million people for a total of US$26 billion. In Mexico, the factoring industry stood at more than US$5 billion in 2004, servicing more than 150,000 small suppliers. In contrast, the number of Chilean companies using factoring is still quite limited, at around 7,000, mostly touching large and medium companies, with an annual turnover of US$5.1 billion. This peculiarity is partially attributed to the weak enforceability of receivables in Chile until recently, and to the recent role of banks in the factoring industry, targeting primarily medium and large enterprises.

Factoring is often ill understood and unregulated, so industry associations are important in policy dialogue and promotion. In Brazil and Chile, factoring firms have an active association, where companies exchanging data about volume of activity work together to call for an improved operating framework.

The Role of the Government in Development of Factoring Activities

Government support of factoring varies across countries. In Mexico, the government-owned Nafin has played an important role in innovation through an e-factoring product (box A4.1). Moreover, Mexican government and public enterprises were pioneers in allowing their small suppliers to factor receivables, with the increased payment discipline this implied. In Chile, the government supports small enterprises through the *fondo de garantía para pequeños empresarios*, which extends factoring and microcredit lines to factoring entities from both banks (US$13 million to 558 medium companies in 2004) and nonbank financial institutions

Figure A4.1. Factoring Turnover in Latin America

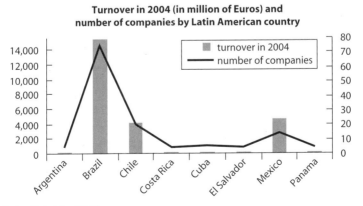

Source: Factors Chain International.

(US$20 million to 3,417 small and microenterprises in 2004). While marginal, these numbers show significant growth compared with 2003.

The development of factoring is significantly strengthened by legislation that clarifies its nature as a transfer of credit, giving judicial strength to the bill sold. For example, factoring companies in Chile are optimistic about the impact of a new law introduced in 2005 that provides judicial strength to bills and clarifies that it is a final sale and transfer of credit. They believe that this measure will increase SME access to this product at lower cost, given that factoring companies can rely more securely on the creditworthiness of the final client. Similarly, the lack of such regulation is one of the obstacles to factoring development in Guatemala and El Salvador.

Governments can enhance the development of the factoring industry through central registries of collateral. Many factoring firms face the risk of fraud through counterfeit receivables, given the lack of central registries of collateral in most Latin American countries. While these risks can be mitigated (through higher premiums, recourse to clients, and screening mechanisms), they usually translate into higher prices and restricted access by some prospective clients.

For taxation purposes, it is usually important to clarify the nature of factoring as the sale of a credit. As such, the sale of the receivable is separate from the sale of goods—it should not be subject to the double imposition of the value added tax or similar taxes, which can make the instrument unattractive. This issue is encountered in Peru and Guatemala.

Some flexibility in the legal definition of the types of documents that can be factored is important. This helps adjustment to country realities in sales practices and widens the universe of factoring activities (international sales documents, sales documents in the informal sector). For example, in Bolivia, there is a restriction by law to factor only exchange bills, a type of receivable that is rarely used in practice. In Guatemala, factoring is limited to goods. Services are excluded.

E-factoring could be promising if necessary laws are adopted. The key success factors for Mexico's Web-based solution were technology and the adoption of laws on electronic signature and security. Several countries might wish to replicate this solution; operators in El Salvador, Guatemala, Peru, and Bolivia have expressed interest.

Several other regulatory and institutional elements favor the development of factoring: a registry of pledged assets to check that receivables are free of liens, effective credit information bureaus, legal frameworks that support creditor rights and provide judicial and extrajudicial restructuring of corporate obligations, and flexible rules on lending rate ceilings.[26]

Annex 4.2. Leasing in Latin America

Leasing is a medium-term financial instrument aimed at covering the investment needs of companies for machinery, equipment, vehicles, and real estate. Leasing institutions (lessors) purchase the equipment, usually as selected by the lessee, and provide the use of equipment to the lessee for a set period. For the duration of the lease, the lessee makes periodic payments to the lessor, with an underlying interest cost. At the end of the lease period, the equipment can be transferred to the ownership of the lessee (typically in financial leasing), returned to the lessor (typically in operational leasing), discarded, or sold to a third party (depending on the characteristics of the contract and the underlying asset).

The benefits of leasing for SMEs are manifold. First, leasing is a tailored instrument to finance investments without making a large initial cash outlay, enabling companies to match expected income and expenditure flows. Accordingly, leasing can increase the productive capacity of the company without affecting significantly its liquidity or leverage levels.[27] Second, leasing contracts can benefit from favorable tax treatment, enabling companies to deduct the leasing monthly expenses from the companies' taxable income.[28] Third, the cost of lease finance is competitive with traditional credit because of the increased security held by lessors.

For financial intermediaries, leasing can be a good instrument to provide financing while assuming lower risks. First, while the risk of default of clients is commensurate to that in bank loans, the loss in case of default can be significantly lower. The repossession and liquidation of the underlying asset is much more rapid, because the ownership of the asset is maintained by the leasing company. Second, the leasing company has reasonable certainty about the value of the asset in a secondary market (in case of repossession) and can price leasing contracts accordingly. Third, leasing by independent operators is subject to lower regulatory oversight than bank loans, hence they face lower regulatory costs and can have leaner processes for credit approval. But, as in the case of factoring, independent leasing companies have a higher cost of funding than banks since they must tap securities markets or borrow from banks.

Until now, leasing has been only a small source of financing in Latin American companies, based on the incomplete available data. A Latin American federation for leasing was established as early as 1985 to promote leasing and its economic, financial, and legal framework. But, with 1.2 percent of worldwide leasing activities in 2003 and an industry that rarely exceeds 0.5 percent of a country's GDP, leasing has remained in an incipient stage in Latin America (figures A4.2 and A4.3). But available statistics on the true size of leasing in Latin America are incomplete because leasing is often unregulated. The true size of these activities could be substantially higher. For example, statistics for Peru severely underestimate the leasing instrument, because it is offered mostly through commercial banks.

Surveys done in the Colombian corporate sector show the relative importance of leasing as a source of capital expenditure, especially for smaller enterprises. Leasing has been a small but visible source of financing for Colombian companies at 3 percent, far behind bank credit and retained earnings. But leasing provided 35 percent of the funding needed for expansion in 2004, considering companies of all sizes. Looking at the picture for SMEs in particular, leasing was even more important, representing more than 40 percent of expansion financing in 2004 (figure A4.4). This finding is valid for the last few years, as illustrated by figure A4.5, showing the evolution of leasing against the total investments by size of enterprise.

There are several reasons for the leasing industry's limited development in Latin America. First, in the absence of specialized leasing laws, judges tend to misunderstand the leasing product, slowing down the recovery of leased assets after default, even though banking laws usually clarify that leasing is distinct from rental and should be governed by the civil code. Second, high informality in the corporate sector can render

Figure A4.2. Overview of Worldwide Leasing Activities

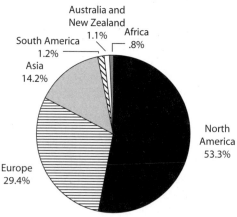

Source: World Leasing Yearbook (2003).

Figure A4.3. Comparison of Leasing Volume to GDP Worldwide

Source: World Leasing Yearbook (2003).

Figure A4.4. Leasing as a Means of Financing Working Capital and Expansion, by Size of Business, 2003 and 2004

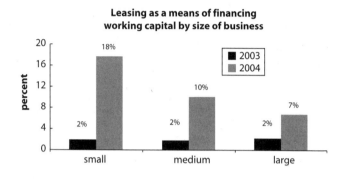

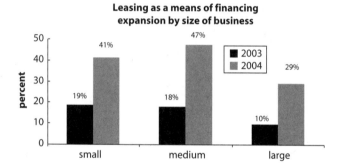

Source: Encuesta de Opinión Empresarial Fedesarrollo—Tamaño de acuerdo a ley 590.

Figure A4.5. Ratio of Leasing to Total Investments, by Size of Business

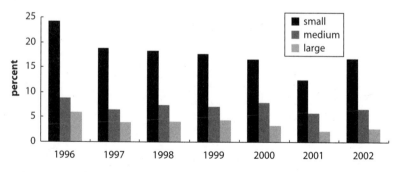

Source: Departamento Administrativo Nacional de Estadística y Superbancaria.

companies insensitive to the fiscal advantages of (operational) leasing. Third, the registry system for assets needs to be improved and enlarged, allowing for a broader variety of assets to be eligible—and for registration to be reliable, efficient, and cost effective. Finally, the high cost of funding is sometimes presented as an obstacle, since leasing tends to be provided by specialized companies that can fund themselves only on the capital markets or through bank credit lines—that is, they are at a disadvantage against commercial banks' cheap funding for collateralized credits.

A full-fledged leasing law is required to address the various obstacles in Latin America. First, this law should make it easier to recover the leased asset in case of lessee default, allowing for extrajudicial processing. Second, the law should clarify the priority of the lessor in case of corporate restructuring or liquidation of the lessee. Third, the law should provide clear accounting and taxation rules, preferably in line with international accounting standards.[29] Other important regulatory and institutional requirements include an efficient and reliable registry system to establish clearly the property right on assets, a wide definition of assets that can be leased,[30] and the possibility of transferring ownership of leasing future flows in securitizations.

Annex 4.3. MFI Loan Securitization: Groundbreaking Transactions[31]

Groundbreaking transactions have recently taken place involving MFIs and their access to domestic and international capital markets. MFI loan securitization is complementing the traditional financing for the MFIs. These transactions provide large amounts of financing at one time, with attractive rates and longer terms, adding to donor contributions. Local and international investors have expressed a strong interest in this new asset class.

The World Bank–FIRST Initiative–National Supervisory Commission for Companies and Securities Technical Assistance Project

A small pilot program is under way in Peru involving securitizing revolving local currency–denominated microloans by some *cajas municipales*—Peru's largest providers of microcredit. The project includes capacity-building efforts, regulatory fine-tuning, and a tentative local currency bond issuance for the equivalent of US$20 million, for which four *cajas municipales* have already applied for a multi-originator approach. The partnership among the World Bank, the multidonor program FIRST Initiative, and the National Supervisory Commission for Companies and Securities could create an interesting model for others in the region.

Multicountry Blue Orchard Securities Transaction

In July 2004, Blue Orchard Securities issued a US$40 million securitization bond of its loans to nine MFIs in Latin America, Eastern Europe, and Asia. The bonds issued had a maturity of seven years and were partially guaranteed by OPIC. The bonds were successfully placed among mainstream institutional investors and individual investors. Another such bond was successfully issued in 2006. But Blue Orchard's securitized loans were in U.S. dollars, while typical MFIs rely increasingly on local currency–denominated funding to reduce credit risk from lending in U.S. dollars to microentrepreneurs whose revenues are in local currency.

Notes

1. Bonds issued in the securities market are usually required to have an independent evaluation of their creditworthiness by a recognized rating agency. Rating scales have levels from AAA to C, progressively denoting lower credit quality.

Ratings are split between investment grade (commonly BBB and above) and subinvestment grade (BB and below). Investment-grade securities are deemed to have a reasonably high probability of being repaid, while subinvestment-grade securities are usually considered high-risk speculative investments.

2. Even in countries with more advanced financial systems, such as Chile, commercial banks usually require collateral in real estate, because the value of movable assets is severely diminished by slow foreclosure processes and the lack of central registries.

3. Notably, the Investment Climate Assessment in Chile pointed out that access to formal financing sources appears higher for microenterprises than for SMEs. Similar results have been observed elsewhere in Latin America. This may be because specific credit processes and products have been developed by banks and specialized lenders to serve microenterprises, while innovation in lending to SMEs has been more limited. This hypothesis has not been tested.

4. When the assets transferred to the market represent a high proportion of the originator's best-performing assets, the risk of the remaining portfolio can be significantly higher, affecting the overall creditworthiness of the originator.

5. In some countries, this problem is exacerbated because financial activities such as factoring and leasing are not sanctioned by law, posing additional constraints for the development of nonbank financial institutions.

6. In contrast, transactions based on "static pools" include assets with long maturities, usually commensurate to that of the overall transaction. This is especially the case for securitization of mortgage loans.

7. Usually, five years or more of historical information is required on default rates in similar portfolios.

8. Traditionally, the data on ultimate recovery in case of loan default are difficult to collect in a standardized way and are scarce even among large banks. This is because the recovery process usually takes a long time and can entail partial writeoffs, partial payments, and foreclosures and sales of assets.

9. Usually, suppliers offer a discount for payment at delivery. The missed discount is the implicit cost of financing for clients that use trade credit instead of prompt payment.

10. This is especially true for captive finance firms, which are financial subsidiaries of manufacturing companies providing credit to clients for purchasing equipment produced by the parent (Ford Credit, GE Capital, GMAC).

11. A recent example was the Mex$80 million issuance of structured bonds by Corporación Metropolitana de Arrendamientos, a Mexican leasing company. However, this transaction was supported by partial credit guarantees provided by Nafin—a local development bank—and the Inter-American Investment Corporation.

12. See annex 4.3 for a summary of MFI securitizations.

13. Financial Security Assurance, a subsidiary of Dexia, is a highly creditworthy insurer of consumer receivable asset-backed securities, residential mortgage-backed securities, collateralized debt obligations, and other structured financings in international markets.

14. For companies securitizing their portfolio of loans, initial commissions and fees on management of the portfolio can be a significant source of income.

15. Banks are required by regulation to hold capital representing a percentage of their credit exposures, which is expected to cover losses suffered by the bank in those operations. Under the forthcoming regulation outlined by international capitalization standards (commonly known as Basel 2 Capital Accord), the percentage of capital required on each credit operation varies according to the credit risk of the borrower—that is, the likelihood that it will default in its obligations. The comparatively high credit risk of SMEs will generate higher capital requirements for banks than lending to other types of borrowers. For SMEs, this can translate into a higher cost of financing and possibly credit rationing among small businesses.

16. For example, commercial banking in many European countries is changing as many banks shift from a business model of buy and hold (retaining all originated loans until maturity) to one of active portfolio management—that is, originating the type of assets whose credit risk can be easily transferred to the market.

17. See "Sistema de garantía de crédito en América Latina: Orientaciones Operativas" by Juan J. Llisterri et al., IADB, 2006.

18. To qualify for an SBA guaranty, a small business must meet eligibility criteria and the lender must certify that it could not provide funding on reasonable terms except with an SBA guaranty. The SBA can then guarantee as much as 85 percent on loans of up to US$150,000 and 75 percent on loans of more than US$150,000. In most cases, the maximum guaranty is US$1 million. Exceptions are the International Trade and 504 loan programs, which have higher loan limits. The maximum total loan size under the 7(a) program is US$2 million. SMEs generally must be operated for profit and fall within the size standards set by the SBA. The SBA determines if the business qualifies as a small business based on the average number of employees during the preceding 12 months or on sales averaged over the previous 3 years. Loans cannot be made to businesses engaged in speculation or investment.

Maximum size standards

- Manufacturing: from 500 to 1,500 employees.
- Wholesaling: 100 employees.
- Services: from US$2.5 million to US$21.5 million in annual receipts.
- Retailing: from US$5 million to US$21 million.

- General construction: from US$13.5 million to US$17 million.
- Special trade construction: average annual receipts not to exceed US$7 million.
- Agriculture: from US$0.5 million to US$9 million.

(*Source:* SBA Guidelines of credit guarantees, http://www.sba.gov/starting_business/startup/guide5.html, March 1, 2007.

19. The fee is based on the maturity of the loan and the dollar amount that the SBA guarantees. On any loan with a maturity of one year or less, the fee is just 0.25 percent of the guaranteed portion of the loan. On loans with maturities of more than one year where the portion that the SBA guarantees is US$80,000 or less, the guaranty fee is 2 percent of the guaranteed portion. On loans with maturities of more than one year where the SBA's portion exceeds US$80,000, the guaranty fee is figured on an incremental scale, beginning at 3 percent.

20. This section draws on the conclusions of Tora (2003).

21. Note that the split of a transaction in various different tranches with different levels of seniority and rating is considered attractive in more developed markets, as it suits different risk appetites for investors. In Latin America, the appeal of differently rated tranches may be more limited.

22. In 1999, the government guaranteed tranches rated AA, A, or BBB. In 2001, only AA- and A-rated tranches were offered the guarantee. In 2003, guarantees were allocated more efficiently, with only AA-rated bonds being eligible for the guarantee.

23. The definition of SMEs used in the program is that of the European Commission—that is, companies with fewer than 250 employees, with annual revenues less than €40 million or total assets less than €27 million, and equity ownership by a large corporation less than 25 percent of the company's capital.

24. Securitization of SME-related assets can be done through true sale or synthetic transactions, with the main difference being whether the ownership of the underlying assets is transferred to the market or remains within the originator. In true sale transactions, the SME loans are segregated from the originator's portfolio and their ownership and credit risk is transferred to a special-purpose vehicle. In synthetic structures, the ownership of the loans remains within the originator's portfolio. Accordingly, the originator does not obtain liquidity, but uses these transactions only to transfer portfolio credit risk to the market.

25. There are three factoring networks in operation worldwide: Factors Chain International, International Factors Group, and Heller International Group.

26. In Peru, the presence of a ceiling on nonbank-lending interest rates slowed the setup of factoring investment funds.

27. Since the leased asset is not the property of the company, it does not increase the assets and liabilities of companies (especially in operational leasing). In fact, many companies sell existing assets to leasing companies and lease them back from them. These operations are known as "lease back" and are done to generate liquidity to be used in further business expansion while maintaining the use of the assets.

28. This is typically the case in operational leasing when the lessee does not plan to retain the ownership of the asset at the end of the contract.

29. In Guatemala, for example, the lack of clear standards agreed on by supervisory and taxation authorities is currently a legal risk that has led to reduced activity by leasing companies.

30. For example, in Guatemala, only movable assets that can be individually identified and registered could be leased—this excludes real estate and nonidentifiable assets.

31. This annex draws on data from Investment's Dealers Digest, the Institute for Financial Management and Research, and the World Bank.

References

Audino, Diane. 2003. "Activos existentes: criterios de Calificación de activos específicos." Standard & Poor's, New York.

Banco de México. 2005. "Encuesta de evaluación coyuntural del mercado crediticio." Mexico City.

Beck, Thorsten, Asli Demirguc-Kunt, and Ross Levine. 2004. "SMEs, Growth, and Poverty." World Bank, Washington, DC.

CIVITAS (Institute for the Study of Civil Society). 2003. "Los fondos de titulización como instrumento alternativo para la financiación de Pymes." London.

de la Torre, Augusto, and Sergio Schmukler. 2004. "Whither Latin American Capital Markets." World Bank, Washington, DC.

de la Torre, Augusto, Juan Carlos Gozzi, and Sergio Schmukler. 2006. "Financial Development in Latin America: Big Emerging Issues, Limited Policy Responses." World Bank, Washington, DC.

Finston, Stroma, Anjali Bastianpillai, and Hervé-Pierre Flammier. 2003. "Standard & Poor's Rating Methodology for CLOs backed by European Small and Mid-Size Enterprise Loans." Standard & Poor's, London.

Gazoni, Pedro, and Cesar Fernandez. 2005. "Fundo de investimento em dereitos creditorios Zoomp." Standard & Poor's, São Paolo, Brazil.

Huettenrauch, Harald. 2004. "Promotion of SME Financing—the Securitization Programme of KfW." Kreditantstalt für Wiederaufbau, Frankfurt, Germany.

IADB (Inter-American Development Bank). 2001. "Acceso de las pequeñas y medianas empresas al financiamiento." Washington, DC.

———. 2003. "IADB Group Support to the SME Sector from 1990–2002." Washington, DC.

Jobst, Andreas. 2002. "Collateralized Loan Obligations—a Primer." Center for Financial Studies, Johann Wolfgang Goethe-Universität, Frankfurt, Germany.

Kabance, Greg, and Samuel Fox. 2005. "Partial-Credit Guarantees Help Improve Recovery Rates in Emerging Markets." Fitch Ratings, New York.

———. 2006. "Structured Finance in Latin America's Local Markets: 2005 Year in Review and 2006 Outlook." Fitch Ratings, New York.

Klapper, Leora. 2004. "The Role of 'Reverse Factoring' in Supplier Financing of Small and Medium-Sized Enterprises." World Bank, Washington, DC.

Klapper, Leora, and Dimitri Vittas. 2003. "The Use of Reverse Factoring." World Bank, Washington, DC.

Kumar, Anjali, and Manuela Francisco. 2005. "Enterprise Size, Financing Patterns, and Credit Constraints in Brazil: Analysis of Data from the Investment Climate Assessment Survey." World Bank, Washington, DC.

Latin American Shadow Financial Regulatory Committee. 2004. "Statement Number 11: Small and Medium-Sized Enterprises Finance in Latin America: Developing Markets, Institutions, and Instruments." Washington, DC.

Llorens, Juan Luis, and Robert Van der Host. 1999. "Compilación de estadísticas en 18 países de América Latina y Caribe." IADB, Washington, DC.

Muller, Maria, and Christian Corcino. 2006. "2005 Review and 2006 Outlook: Latin American ABS/MBS Domestic Market Issuance Drives the Growth, While Cross Border Issuance Takes a Backseat." Moody's Investors Service, New York.

Ossa, Felipe. 2005. "Zoomp to Show Markets Its Assets." Asset Securitization Report, Securitization.Net, Chicago, IL.

Ramos, Jan Smith. 2003. "Financing SMEs in Latin America—Waking Up to the Opportunity." Infoamericas, Miami.

Rubio, Giancarlo. 2006. "Internacional de títulos Sociedad Titulizadora, S.A. Bonos Titulizados Grupo Drokasa." Equilibrium Clasificadora de Riesgo, Lima.

Standard & Poor's. 2004. "Primera emisión de certificados bursátiles estructurados del primer programa de Servicios Financieros Navistar con créditos para la adquisición de equipos de transporte." Mexico City.

———. 2005. "Fundo de investimento em dereitos creditorios Zoomp." São Paolo.

———.2006. "Structured Finance Emerging Markets Ratings Lists." New York.

Tello, Mauricio, and Sergio Figueroa. 2006. "Segunda emisión de certificados bursátiles de Corporación Metropolitana de Arrendamientos con garantías parciales de Nafin y la CII." Standard & Poor's, Mexico City.

Tora, Jose. 2003. "Spanish Securitization Market Set for 30 Percent Growth in 2003." Standard & Poor's, Madrid.

United Nations. 2004. "Meeting the Challenges in an Era of Globalization by Strengthening Regional Development Cooperation." Economic and Social Commission for Asia and the Pacific, New York.

Watanabe, Roberto. 2005. "The Evolution of FIDCs in Brazilian Securitization." Moody's Investors Service, New York.

World Bank. 2005a. "Investment Climate Assessment—Brazil." Washington, DC.

———. 2005b. "Investment Climate Assessment—El Salvador." Washington, DC.

———. Forthcoming. "Investment Climate Assessment—Chile." Washington, DC.

Zervos, Sara. 2004. "The Transaction Costs of Primary Market Issuance: The Case of Brazil, Chile, and Mexico." World Bank, Washington, DC.

Asset Securitization

This annex presents a short overview of securitization, its benefits to issuers and investors, and the basic legal, regulatory, and market infrastructure for securitization transactions.

What Is Securitization?

Securitization involves structuring and packaging a pool of cash flow–generating, underlying assets (receivables, mortgage loans, future revenues) into marketable securities, which are then sold to investors. In almost all cases, a special-purpose vehicle is created to purchase the assets, which it does by issuing securities (such as bonds) in its own name. By this process, the risk associated with the initial owner and seller of the cash-generating assets is removed from the risk inherent in the underlying assets. Investors who purchase the bonds issued by the special-purpose vehicle rely on the credit quality of the special-purpose vehicle, which depends on the future cash flow of the cash-generating assets—not on the credit quality of the initial owner and seller of the assets.

Conceptually, securitization is analogous to collateralized borrowing. When an entity borrows, repayment of the loan can be guaranteed by pledging certain assets as collateral. Similarly, when securitization takes

Figure App. 1.1. A Typical Asset Securitization Transaction

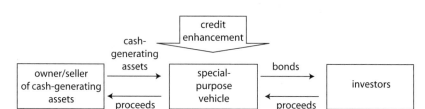

place, the initial borrowing (issuance of bonds) is guaranteed by pledging future cash flows as collateral, with those future cash flows backing the future interest and principal repayment (figure A1.1). For this reason, securitization is often described as creating asset-backed securities.

Securitization is a form of credit disintermediation, since institutions in need of funding can access financial markets directly by securitizing their cash flow–generating assets without the need to borrow from traditional commercial banks. It "liquefies" cash flow–generating assets, turning them—through the bonds backed by these assets—into tradable securities that can be bought and sold by investors in the capital markets. It can thus be defined as the transformation of illiquid assets into a security that can be issued and traded in a capital market. It can also be seen as a process of redistributing economic risks among participants in the transaction according to their appetite for risk and expertise in risk management.

Securitization can develop domestic capital markets. The legal, supervisory, and regulatory frameworks and the financial expertise and multiplicity of agents necessary tend to act as catalysts for additional financial instruments, increasing the breadth and depth of domestic capital markets.

Benefits of Securitization

Securitization brings benefits to both issuers and investors:

- Diversification of funding sources.
- New or improved access to capital markets.
- Lower cost of funds than commercial bank borrowing.
- A means to free capital for redeployment or reinvestment in profitable businesses.
- Reduced credit exposure to the relevant cash-generating underlying assets.

- Improved asset and liability management, thanks to a better match of funding and lending maturities.
- Flexible investment opportunities tailored to match yield, liquidity, and credit quality requirements.

Participants in Securitization

A typical securitization transaction requires the involvement and interaction of many agents:

- *Owner/seller.* The true originator of the transaction, whose incentive is to raise additional funding by leveraging the underlying cash-generating assets it owns.
- *Special-purpose vehicle.* An independent legal entity specifically created to hold the underlying assets until the maturity of the financing.
- *Credit enhancer.* An entity or process that increases the creditworthiness of the underlying assets and improves the marketability of the bonds to be issued.
- *Rating agency.* An institution whose mission is to assess the creditworthiness of the underlying assets and the securitization structure; it assigns a credit rating to the bonds to be issued.
- *Underwriter.* A financial institution marketing and distributing the bonds to be issued.
- *Investors.* Purchasers and holders of the bonds issued by the special-purpose vehicle.
- *Servicer.* When needed, an entity is responsible for the recovery of the assets securitized. For example, in loans securitization, the originating financial institution will typically continue to service these loans through monitoring and recovery.

Asset-backed securities are designed and structured to isolate the cash flow–generating assets from the credit standing of the owner and seller. To achieve complete independence, the cash-generating assets are sold to a separate legal entity (the special-purpose vehicle), which, as a legally independent entity, is generally no longer influenced by the credit quality of the initial owner and seller of the underlying assets. So, even if the seller of the cash-generating assets were to file for bankruptcy, the underlying cash-generating assets would not be affected.

Once securitization has taken place, the credit standing of the pool of underlying assets is dependent exclusively on the inherent quality of the assets themselves. There are exceptions. One is when a financial institutional securitizes a portfolio of loans but retains the responsibility for recovery of loan installments. Another is when the securitization is done with recourse to the issuer, or when the issuer is responsible for renewing the pool of assets as they mature, if the securitization bond has a longer maturity than the underlying assets.

In its simplest form, securitization through a special-purpose vehicle is designed as a pass-through. The special-purpose vehicle is a passive entity that owns the underlying assets and that transfers (passes though) the performance of such assets to fulfill the payment obligations on the bonds initially issued.

Credit Enhancement

Once the cash flow–generating assets have been transferred to the legally independent special-purpose vehicle, techniques are typically used to enhance the credit quality of the special-purpose vehicle. Note that the cash flow–generating assets generally constitute the sole assets of the special-purpose vehicle, so the overall credit quality of the special-purpose vehicle depends only on the quality of the assets and on the credit quality of other entities that may support the credit quality of the special purpose vehicle. To maximize its credit quality, the special-purpose vehicle uses techniques to structure the underlying cash-generating assets. There are typically two main types of credit enhancements: internal and external.

Internal Credit Enhancement

Senior-subordinated structure. Under this arrangement, investors holding the senior bonds have the first claim on payments generated by the pool of underlying assets, while investors holding the subordinated bonds have a junior (lower) claim. So senior-class bonds enjoy a higher rating than junior-class bonds (the chance of default is lower), while holders of junior-class bonds face less certain repayment. Consistent with their lower risk profile, senior-class bonds have a lower rate of return than junior-class bonds.

Overcollateralized structure. Another structuring technique to enhance the credit of the special-purpose vehicle would be to transfer a pool of assets with a face value larger than the face value of the initial bond issuance. A "cushion" within the pool of assets of the special purpose vehicle ensures the full payment of the interest and principal of the initial bond issuance. Once repayment is complete, the remaining assets in the special-purpose vehicle revert to the initial seller.

External Credit Enhancement

Partial credit guarantee. Partial credit guarantees are credit enhancement instruments provided by commercial security assurance companies, public entities such as development banks, and multilateral organisms. Partial credit guarantees can be acquired and structured to either reduce the probability of default (when the guarantee is intended to cover liquidity problems) or enhance recovery in case of default (when the guarantee is intended to cover shortfalls after the resources from the securitized assets have been used). An originator can reduce the proportion of the subordinated tranche in a transaction by purchasing partial credit guarantees. However, using these mechanisms does not necessarily reduce the cost to the originator. For example, if the market is efficient, the guarantee fee will equal the difference between the yields of the senior bonds and those of the subordinated bonds. However, partial credit guarantees can make a transaction more appealing to investors.

Seller guarantee or recourse to seller. As in overcollateralization, the initial seller of the cash-generating assets commits to transfer additional assets to the special-purpose vehicle if there is a shortfall in the initial assets that backed the issuance of bonds. This structure does not completely isolate the special-purpose vehicle from the credit standing of the initial seller, since the recourse mechanism depends on the capacity of the initial seller to honor its commitment.

Hedging. Another mechanism for the special-purpose vehicle to insulate itself from certain risks is to hedge part or all of those risks by purchasing hedging products such as credit derivatives or put options.

Legal, Tax, and Financial Underpinnings

For securitization transactions to occur and prosper, the environment must enable the proper structuring of the transaction and the adequate alignment of economic interests among the multiplicity of agents in the securitization market.

Credit Rating of Securitization Transactions

To attract investors to purchase the asset-backed securities, rating agencies (such as Standard & Poor's, Moody's, and Fitch) provide an official rating of the bonds issued, depending on the credit quality achieved through the credit-enhancement techniques. This credit rating takes into account the likely performance of the underlying assets (under best- and worst-case scenarios) and the likely effect on those assets of changing overall market conditions.

Legal Issues

Three legal issues in a securitization transaction are the independence of the special-purpose vehicle, the legal conditions in which the special-purpose vehicle has been created, and the manner of transferring assets from the owner/seller to the special-purpose vehicle.

The special-purpose vehicle's independence is essential to ensure its bankruptcy remoteness. The special-purpose vehicle needs to sever the original relationship with the owner/seller of the underlying assets and to delink itself from the originator's creditworthiness. In addition, restrictions are needed on the special-purpose vehicle to ensure that it fulfills the actions for which it has been created as they relate to the management of the underlying assets. This precondition can also be expanded to include clear bankruptcy procedures to ensure that, if they become necessary, the true value of the underlying assets can be efficiently transferred to its ultimate beneficial owners.

The legal standing, personality, and corporate form of the special-purpose vehicle affects the transfer of the intrinsic economic value of the underlying assets to its ultimate beneficial owners. The special-purpose vehicle only owns the underlying assets on behalf of the bondholders—not in place of them. This creates a need for special legislation (typically called trust legislation) allowing for such understanding to be formally undertaken without conflicting with existing legislation (the civil code, for example) that includes a different definition of ownership.

To underscore the special-purpose vehicle's independence and bankruptcy remoteness, the initial sale of the assets from the owner/seller to the special-purpose vehicle needs to be perfected as a true sale, without the possibility of recourse in the event of bankruptcy of the owner/seller. Securitization can occur only when such a sale is legally considered final, binding, and irreversible.

Tax Issues

Tax frameworks can also be obstacles to securitizing assets, because the transfer of such assets is often taxed. Securitization does not change the substance of the underlying assets, whose new owner (the special-purpose vehicle) is simply an empty shell designed to pass through the economic value of the underlying assets. So, it is essential to ensure the tax neutrality of the special-purpose vehicle and not to use securitization as an opportunity (or excuse) to tax an activity that should not be subject to additional taxation. Existing tax codes often choose to ignore this fact, resulting in additional taxation, which—by increasing the cost—prevents securitization from flourishing.

Financial and Other Issues

The predictability of the cash flow to be generated by the underlying assets helps reduce uncertainty and risk. This helps in pricing securitization transactions and reducing structuring costs. The homogeneity of the underlying assets and the standardization of documentation for those assets also reduce uncertainty and lower costs. And as with many other financial assets, a reliable, market-driven yield curve for valuing the underlying assets is essential—not only for the initial structuring and pricing, but also to serve as a benchmark for pricing evolution and comparisons throughout the life of the transaction. Also essential is accounting for transactions to reflect the true ownership of the underlying assets (and their future cash flow), the independence of the special-purpose vehicle, and the contractual obligation underpinning the bonds issued.

Statistics on Financial Markets in Latin America and Selected Comparator Countries

Table A.1. Deposit Money Bank Credit to the Private Sector
(percent of GDP)

Country	1995	2000	2001	2002	2003	2004
Latin America and the Caribbean						
Argentina	20	23	20	15	11	10
Bolivia	47	51	46	42	39	33
Brazil	33	28	29	28	29	28
Chile	54	62	63	63	61	61
Colombia	18	19	19	20	20	19
Costa Rica	11	24	28	30	31	32
El Salvador	4	5	5	5	5	5
Mexico	29	17	15	17	15	14
Peru	16	26	24	23	20	18
Uruguay	26	51	54	66	44	30
Eastern Europe						
Czech Rep.	71	48	40	30	31	32
Hungary	22	32	34	36	43	47.
Poland	17	27	28	28	29	28
East Asia and the Pacific						
Indonesia	53	21	20	22	24	23
Korea, Rep. of	50	79	84	92	95	89
Malaysia	83	94	101	99	97	105
Western Europe						
Portugal	69	—	—	—	—	—
Spain	74	—	—	—	—	—

Sources: International Monetary Fund International Financial Statistics database and World Bank.

— not available.

Table A.2. Government Debt Securities Outstanding
(percent of GDP)

Country	1995	2000	2001	2002	2003	2004
Latin America and the Caribbean						
Argentina	9	12	9	5	7	6
Bolivia	—	—	—	—	—	—
Brazil	18	41	51	37	50	49
Chile	—	—	—	—	—	—
Colombia	—	—	—	—	—	—
Costa Rica	—	—	—	—	—	—
El Salvador	—	—	—	—	—	—
Mexico	6	10	12	18	21	23
Peru	—	—	—	—	—	—
Uruguay	—	—	—	—	—	—
Eastern Europe						
Czech Rep.	16	32	34	52	55	54
Hungary	26	33	36	—	—	—
Poland	18	19	24	29	31	40
East Asia and the Pacific						
Indonesia	—	—	—	—	—	—
Korea, Rep. of	8	14	16	15	19	25
Malaysia	—	31	36	36	39	40
Thailand	—	21	26	23	21	22
Western Europe						
Portugal	43	36	37	49	53	57
Spain	48	50	46	51	48	45

Sources: Bank for International Settlements and World Bank.

— not available.

Table A.3. Market Capitalization
(percent of GDP)

Country	1995	2000	2001	2002	2003	2004	2005[a]
Latin America and the Caribbean							
Argentina	15	58	72	101	30	31	41
Bolivia	—	—	—	—	—	—	—
Brazil	21	38	37	27	48	55	59
Chile	113	80	85	71	119	124	141
Colombia	19	11	16	12	18	26	36
Costa Rica	5	—	—	—	3	3	—
Mexico	32	22	20	16	20	25	29
Peru	22	20	21	24	27	29	35
Uruguay	7	—	—	—	—	—	—
Eastern Europe							
Czech Rep.	28	20	15	22	20	29	31
Hungary	5	26	20	20	20	29	34
Poland	3	19	14	15	18	29	29
East Asia and the Pacific							
Indonesia	33	18	16	17	26	28	27
Korea, Rep. of	35	29	46	46	54	63	75
Malaysia	251	129	136	130	162	161	139
Thailand	84	24	31	36	83	70	72
Western Europe							
Portugal	17	57	42	—	—	—	—
Spain	26	90	80	70	87	95	93

Sources: Standard & Poor's Emerging Markets Data Base, International Federation of Stock Exchanges, International Monetary Fund, and World Bank.

— not available.

a. Derived using end-September data from the Emerging Markets Data Base (International Federation of Stock Exchanges for Spain) and GDP forecasts from the International Monetary Fund's World Economic Outlook database.

Table A.4. Shares Traded

(percent of GDP)

Country	1995	2000	2001	2002	2003	2004	2005[a]
Latin America and the Caribbean							
Argentina	1.8	2.1	1.6	1.3	3.8	5.0	9.6
Bolivia	—	—	—	—	—	—	—
Brazil	11.2	16.8	12.8	10.5	12.3	15.5	18.1
Chile	17.0	8.1	6.4	4.6	9.0	12.3	18.2
Colombia	1.4	0.5	0.4	0.3	0.5	1.5	4.3
Costa Rica	0.1	—	—	—	0.7	0.8	—
El Salvador	—	—	—	—	—	—	—
Mexico	12.0	7.8	6.4	4.3	3.8	6.3	6.7
Peru	7.3	2.9	1.6	2.0	1.3	1.6	1.6
Uruguay	0.0	—	—	—	—	—	—
Eastern Europe							
Czech Rep.	6.6	11.8	5.5	8.2	9.8	16.5	34.9
Hungary	0.8	26.0	9.3	9.2	10.0	13.0	21.2
Poland	2.0	8.8	4.0	3.1	4.1	6.9	9.9
East Asia and the Pacific							
Indonesia	7.1	9.5	6.8	7.5	7.1	10.7	17.4
Korea, Rep. of	35.8	208.6	146.1	144.9	112.8	94.0	130.9
Malaysia	86.5	64.8	23.6	29.0	48.3	50.8	41.1
Thailand	33.9	19.0	30.9	37.6	67.6	66.7	57.4
Western Europe							
Portugal	3.9	51.6	—	—	—	—	—
Spain	—	—	—	99.7	111.3	121.4	141.4

Sources: Standard & Poor's Emerging Markets Data Base, International Federation of Stock Exchanges, International Monetary Fund, and World Bank.

— not available.

a. Calculated by annualizing monthly trading data through September and dividing by the forecasted 2005 GDP obtained from the International Monetary Fund's World Economic Outlook database.

Table A.5. Pension Fund Assets
(percent of GDP)

Country	1995	2000	2001	2002	2003	2004
Latin America and the Caribbean						
Argentina	1	7	8	11	12	12
Bolivia	—	10	12	15	19	20
Brazil	—	—	—	10	13	—
Chile	39	48	53	53	69	65
Colombia	0	4	6	7	9	11
Costa Rica	—	—	0	1	2	3
El Salvador	—	4	6	7	11	14
Mexico	—	3	4	5	6	6
Peru	1	6	7	8	10	11
Uruguay	—	4	6	7	11	13
Eastern Europe						
Czech Rep.	0	2	2	3	3	—
Hungary	0	3	4	5	5	—
Poland	—	1	2	4	5	6
East Asia and the Pacific						
Indonesia	—	—	2	3	2	—
Korea, Rep. of	3	2	—	2	2	—
Malaysia	—	—	—	—	56	—
Thailand	—	—	8	8	7	—
Western Europe						
Portugal	8	11	12	12	12	—
Spain	5	9	6	6	7	—

Sources: Association of Latin American Pension Supervisors, International Federation of Pension Funds Administrators, Organisation for Economic Co-operation and Development, and World Bank.

— not available.

Table A.6. Insurance Assets
(percent of GDP)

Country	1995	2000	2001	2002	2003	2004
Latin America and the Caribbean						
Argentina	—	4	5	—	—	—
Bolivia	—	—	—	—	—	—
Brazil	—	3	4	—	—	—
Chile	—	16	20	20	25	—
Colombia	—	3	4	—	—	—
Costa Rica	—	—	—	—	—	—
El Salvador	—	—	—	—	—	—
Mexico	1	3	3	3	4	—
Peru	—	2	2	—	—	—
Uruguay	—	—	—	—	—	—
Eastern Europe						
Czech Rep.	5	7	—	—	—	—
Hungary	3	5	—	—	—	—
Poland	1	4	—	—	—	—
East Asia and the Pacific						
Indonesia	—	—	—	—	—	—
Korea, Rep. of	21	27	—	—	—	—
Malaysia	—	—	—	—	—	—
Thailand	—	—	—	—	—	—
Western Europe						
Portugal	11	20	25	23	20	—
Spain	13	18	19	22	15	—

Sources: Organisation for Economic Co-operation and Development, Association of Insurance Supervisors of Latin America, and World Bank.

— not available.

Table A.7. Factoring Volume
(percent of GDP)

Country	1995	2000	2001	2002	2003	2004
Latin America and the Caribbean						
Argentina	—	0.6	0.3	0.1	0.1	—
Bolivia	—	—	—	—	—	—
Brazil	—	1.8	1.9	2.3	2.8	—
Chile	—	3.2	4.2	4.4	5.5	—
Colombia	—	0.0	0.0	0.0	0.0	—
Costa Rica	—	1.5	1.1	1.2	1.2	—
El Salvador	—	—	0.8	1.0	0.8	—
Mexico	—	0.8	1.0	0.9	0.8	—
Peru	—	—	—	—	—	—
Uruguay	—	—	—	—	—	—
Eastern Europe						
Czech Rep.	—	1.7	1.8	2.1	2.4	—
Hungary	—	0.7	0.9	0.8	1.6	—
Poland	—	1.2	1.6	1.2	1.4	—
East Asia and the Pacific						
Indonesia	—	0.0	0.0	0.0	0.0	—
Korea, Rep. of	—	0.0	0.0	0.0	0.0	—
Malaysia	—	0.6	0.9	0.6	0.8	—
Thailand	—	1.0	1.0	0.9	1.1	—
Western Europe						
Portugal	—	7.8	8.3	8.8	9.3	—
Spain	—	3.2	3.6	4.5	5.0	—

Sources: Factors Chain International and World Bank.

— not available.

Table A.8. Leasing Assets
(percent of GDP)

Country	1995	2000	2001	2002	2003	2004
Latin America and the Caribbean						
Argentina	—	—	0.2	—	—	—
Bolivia	—	—	—	—	—	—
Brazil	—	—	0.7	0.4	0.4	—
Chile	—	—	0.5	0.6	0.7	—
Colombia	—	—	0.9	0.9	1.0	—
Costa Rica	—	—	—	0.8	1.0	—
El Salvador	—	—	—	—	—	—
Mexico	—	—	0.1	0.2	0.3	—
Peru	—	—	1.0	0.9	0.9	—
Uruguay	—	—	—	—	—	—
Eastern Europe						
Czech Rep.	—	—	4.3	3.5	4.5	—
Hungary	—	—	3.7	4.0	4.6	—
Poland	—	—	1.1	1.3	1.4	—
East Asia and the Pacific						
Indonesia	—	—	0.2	—	0.7	—
Korea, Rep. of	—	—	0.2	0.4	0.4	—
Malaysia	—	—	—	0.3	0.4	—
Thailand	—	—	0.3	—	—	—
Western Europe						
Portugal	—	—	2.4	2.1	1.9	—
Spain	—	—	1.3	1.4	1.4	—

Sources: Euromoney and World Bank.

— not available.

Table A.9. Mutual Fund Assets

(percent of GDP)

Country	1995	2000	2001	2002	2003	2004
Latin America and the Caribbean						
Argentina	—	3	1	1	1	—
Bolivia	—	—	—	—	—	—
Brazil	—	25	29	21	35	—
Chile	—	6	8	10	12	—
Colombia	—	—	—	—	—	—
Costa Rica	—	6	10	10	16	—
El Salvador	—	—	—	—	—	—
Mexico	—	3	5	5	5	—
Peru	—	—	—	—	—	—
Uruguay	—	—	—	—	—	—
Eastern Europe						
Czech Rep.	—	4	3	4	5	—
Hungary	—	4	4	6	5	—
Poland	—	1	2	3	4	—
East Asia and the Pacific						
Indonesia	—	—	—	—	—	—
Korea, Rep. of	—	22	25	27	20	—
Malaysia	—	—	—	—	—	—
Thailand	—	—	—	—	—	—
Western Europe						
Portugal	—	16	15	16	18	—
Spain	—	31	27	27	30	—

Sources: Investment Company Institute and World Bank.

— not available.

Table A.10. Getting Credit

Country	Legal rights index[a] (0 = low, 10 = high)	Credit information index[b] (0 = low, 10 = high)	Public registry coverage (percent of adults)	Private bureau coverage (percent of adults)
Latin America and the Caribbean				
Argentina	3	6	22.1	95
Bolivia	3	4	10.3	24.6
Brazil	2	5	9.6	53.6
Chile	4	6	45.7	22.1
Colombia	4	4	0	31.7
Costa Rica	4	6	34.8	4.5
El Salvador	5	5	17.3	78.7
Mexico	2	6	0	49.4
Peru	2	6	30.2	27.8
Uruguay	4	5	5.5	80
Eastern Europe				
Czech Rep.	6	5	2.8	37.9
Hungary	6	5	0	4
Poland	3	4	0	38.1
East Asia and the Pacific				
Indonesia	5	3	0	0.1
Korea, Rep. of	8	6	33.7	—
Malaysia	6	5	0	80.7
Thailand	5	4	0	18.4
Western Europe				
Portugal	5	4	64.3	9.8
Spain	5	6	42.1	6.5

Sources: World Bank, Doing Business database.

— not available.

a. Higher scores indicate that collateral and bankruptcy laws are better designed to expand access to credit.

b. Higher values indicate that more credit information is available from a public registry or a private bureau to facilitate lending decisions.

Index

ECO-AUDIT
Environmental Benefits Statement

The World Bank is committed to preserving endangered forests and natural resources. The Office of the Publisher has chosen to print *Structured Finance in Latin America* on 60# paper including 30% post-consumer recycled fiber in accordance with the recommended standards for paper usage set by the Green Press Initiative, a nonprofit program supporting publishers in using fiber that is not sourced from endangered forests. For more information, visit www.greenpressinitiative.org.

Saved:

- 5 trees
- 3 million BTUs of total energy
- 408 lbs. of net greenhouse gases
- 1,692 gallons of water
- 217 lbs. of solid waste